# dissertation

What you need to know and how to do it

Bill Kirton

**Prentice Hall**
is an imprint of

**PEARSON**

Harlow, England • London • New York • Boston • San Francisco • Toronto • Sydney • Singapore • Hong Kong
Tokyo • Seoul • Taipei • New Delhi • Cape Town • Madrid • Mexico City • Amsterdam • Munich • Paris • Milan

**PEARSON EDUCATION LIMITED**

Edinburgh Gate
Harlow CM20 2JE
Tel: +44 (0)1279 623623
Fax: +44 (0)1279 431059
Website: www.pearsoned.co.uk

First published in Great Britain in 2011

ISBN: 978-0-273-74377-4

British Library Cataloguing-in-Publication Data
A catalogue record for this book is available from the British Library

Library of Congress Cataloging-in-Publication Data
Kirton, Bill.
 Brilliant dissertation / Bill Kirton.
  p. cm.
 Includes bibliographical references.
 ISBN 978-0-273-74377-4 (pbk.)
 1. Dissertations, Academic--handbooks, manuals, etc. 2. Academic writing--
Handbooks, manuals, etc. I. Title
 LB2369.K534 2011
 808'.02--dc22

                                                                    2010046057

10 9 8 7 6 5 4 3 2 1
14 13 12 11 10

Typeset in 10/14pt Plantin by 3
Printed in Great Britain by Henry Ling Ltd., at the Dorset Press, Dorchester,
Dorset

# Contents

# About the author

Before taking early retirement to become a full-time writer, **Bill Kirton** was a lecturer in French at the University of Aberdeen. He has also been a Royal Literary Fund Writing Fellow at the RGU in Aberdeen, and the universities of Dundee and St Andrews. His radio plays have been broadcast by the BBC and on the Australian BC. His crime novels and a historical novel have been published in the UK and USA and his short stories have appeared in several anthologies. He lives in Aberdeen with his wife, Carolyn.

His website is www.bill-kirton.co.uk and his blog is at http://livingwritingandotherstuff.blogspot.com/

# Acknowledgements

I owe a lot to the students I've worked with over the years. I hope I taught them some things; I know they taught me many. So let me acknowledge at the start my appreciation of the interesting and stimulating discussions I shared with them. More specifically in the context of this volume, I'd like to thank Steve Cook and others at the Royal Literary Fund who initiated and ran the imaginative scheme which funded Writing Fellowships in universities throughout the UK. It was through that scheme that I met Kathleen McMillan and Jonathan Weyers, who became friends as well as colleagues. My thanks to them for their expertise, knowledge, experience and friendship and to Dr Steve Lakin for his helpful mathematical advice. Finally, Steve Temblett, Katy Robinson and Natasha Whelan at Pearson Education have been unfailingly kind and cooperative and I'm truly grateful to them for all their help.

## Publisher's acknowledgements

We are grateful to the following for permission to reproduce copyright material:

Table 23.1 Adapted from Table 1 'Marks for copy preparation and proof correction' BS 5261-2:2005, British Standards Institution. Permission to reproduce extracts from BS 5261-2:2005 is granted by BSI. No other use of this material is permitted. British Standards can be obtained in PDF or hard copy formats from the BSI online shop: www.bsigroup.com/Shop

or by contacting BSI Customer Services for hard copy only: Tel: +44 (0)208 996 9001, email: cservices@bsigroup.com

In some instances we have been unable to trace the owners of copyright material, and we would appreciate any information that would enable us to do so.

# Introduction: Do as we say not as we do

To explain why we chose that heading for the introduction, let's start with a question. What's wrong with these sentences (all of which you'll find in this book)?

1 Another obvious format.
2 But dissertations and reports are long-term affairs and that brings its own problems.
3 And yet, in a few months, you'll be handing in a substantial document on it which is all your own work.
4 After you've told them what's involved ...
5 The main thing to consider is who you're writing them for.

The main answer is that they all break rules (of grammar, punctuation and style) which we'll be saying must *never* be broken. (As does that sentence, too, because we're not 'saying' anything, we're 'writing' it.) More specifically, 1 isn't a sentence because there's no verb in it; 2 and 3 begin with conjunctions, i.e. words which should join two parts of a sentence, not start it; 4 uses contractions ('you've' and 'what's'); and 5 ends with a preposition and 'who' should be 'whom'.

Another question – this time about the whole problem of political correctness and gender-specific language. When we give examples involving a student or lecturer, do we say he or she? Or do we stay correct, use the either/or form and write sentences such as 'The student must ensure that he or she conducts his or her research in a style that suits himself or herself'? We hope the answer to that one is self-evident.

The reason we're starting with these questions is to warn you against copying the style of this book in your academic writing; it breaks lots of the rules which you'll need to respect. Why? Because our aim here isn't to be academic or formal; we want our style to be personal, conversational, direct and easy to read. So we don't mind starting paragraphs with 'OK', or sentences with 'And', 'But' or 'Because'. We'll be using the sort of contractions familiar in everyday speech, such as 'you'll', 'we've' and 'don't'. We don't want the writing to be sloppy or give you examples of 'bad' English but nor do we want to be constrained by the formality of conventional academic style.

So that's why we've used the 'incorrect' formulae in the sentences we quoted. And the way we'll overcome the gender-specific issue is by using 'he' or 'she' at random. Students and lecturers alike will sometimes be male, sometimes female. There'll be no attempt to make sure there's a fifty-fifty split to guarantee political correctness either. Our intention throughout isn't to be 'correct' but to communicate.

The book's organised in eight parts. The first is a general introduction on getting started and choosing a topic. Part 2 is about planning your research, while Part 3 deals with finding and filtering information. In Part 4 we look at research techniques, Part 5 deals with issues arising from data and numbers and Part 6 addresses the important topics of plagiarism, referencing and ethics. Part 7 focuses on the actual writing of your dissertation or project report and the last part is devoted to editing and presenting the final work.

You'll find that some points, such as those concerning referencing and plagiarism, the need to stay objective and the importance of using evidence to support your arguments are repeated quite frequently. We've done this deliberately whenever we feel something needs to be stressed or re-stressed.

When you've read the book, if it's helped you to feel more confident about things, we've achieved our goal. University is a great foundation for your future and completing a research project is an excellent way of developing and demonstrating your abilities and finding out more about yourself in the process.

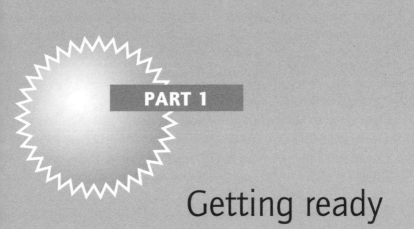

**PART 1**

# Getting ready

**CHAPTER 1**

# The challenges

Dissertations and project reports are demanding tasks in terms of both research and writing. They're the sort of exercises that often come later in a degree course or at postgraduate level, but many institutions now make them an earlier part of the learning process. They can have a noticeable effect on your marks and, possibly, influence your overall classification.

## A professional approach

Imagine looking at a substantial piece of work on a topic that interests you. It's a bound volume of several thousand words and there, on the cover page, is your name. For many students, it's one of the highlights of their undergraduate academic career. It's taken them a few months to put together but it's proof that they have the knowledge, understanding and, not least, stamina to make their own choices, follow them through and show that they've mastered the advanced academic skills of their discipline.

OK, you've imagined it, now how do you set about making it a reality? Well, in broad terms, you'll have to choose your topic, do lots of research, thinking and writing and you'll have to present it all in a professional way. And it'll be your unique, original contribution to your subject. You'll get well under the surface of your material and have to push yourself to meet the various challenges it'll present. The skills involved may be close to those that potential employers will be looking for, too. So, in every way, it's clear that you need to treat such tasks with energy, commitment and a determination to show how focused and disciplined you can be.

> ## brilliant tip
>
> Writing dissertations and project reports are similar activities in many ways, but there are differences, too. Wherever possible, we've tried to provide material which applies to both, but there are also chapters and sections that focus on techniques and strategies for specific types of document. Find the material which best suits your own needs and meets the requirements of your particular discipline.

## Getting a good start

Exercises such as essays, lab reports and case studies are relatively short-term commitments, with usually a few weeks or even days between the exercise being set and the submission date. But dissertations and reports are long-term affairs and that brings its own problems. With a whole term or more in which to complete the task, it's easy to drift aimlessly at the start and just convince yourself that thinking vaguely about the topic now and then keeps you in touch with it. It doesn't. Students who've written their dissertations often remark that each stage took longer than they expected. So don't be under any illusions; if you don't get organised, the time will rush by and you'll be struggling to meet the deadlines.

good time management is critical

Good time management is critical. As soon as you know what the task is, focus on it, start planning the various elements and make it a part of your routines. The sooner you start, the sooner you'll experience the reality of the job in hand and the more inclined you'll be to commit to something that's exclusively yours. So, do something positive.

- Find out (and make sure you understand) exactly what it is you're supposed to do and how you should do it. Read the course handbook or regulations or talk to your supervisor or, if you don't yet have one, someone who might be your supervisor.

- Start looking at your research area or source material. It'll probably seem vast at first, with jargon that maybe sounds obscure, and you may feel that so many experts have written so much on it that you can't imagine finding anything to add. And yet, in a few months, you'll be handing in a substantial document on it which is all your own work. So get involved in the topic, start reading some background material and start asking questions. The sooner you start, the better.

- Sitting thinking about it is part of the process, but at this stage you should also be active. Start taking focused notes of your background reading, create a plan of action, organise your timetable. In some research projects, you may have to make some early observations or set up a pilot experiment; in others, you may need to source materials and/or textbooks. Whatever initial things your task calls for, get stuck into them.

## brilliant tip

Check your motivation. Your friends, family and tutors may all think you're motivated but you're the only one who really knows.

- If you are, use the feeling to get yourself energised and tap into it whenever things get difficult.

- If you're not, talk to someone about it. Some supervisors are very good at motivating students, and staff in support services such as counselling and the careers service also have lots of experience of helping in this way.

## Work efficiently and effectively

In the course of the book we'll keep stressing the need to organise your timetable. It makes sense; you won't lose or waste time worrying about what you should be doing or whether you're on track, and you'll have more time not only for thinking and reading but also for relaxing. So get into the habit of being efficient.

- Plan ahead for each day or part of a day.
- Make sure you know precisely what you're trying to achieve during each day or part of a day.
- Get working as quickly as possible.
- Prioritise tasks.
- Don't get distracted.
- Keep your papers and your workplace well organised.
- Don't overdo it. Take breaks when you need to rest.

As well as efficient, be effective. That means doing things that actually produce results. Be sure that each thing you do has a point and is contributing in some way to achieving your goal.

- Don't waste time. Get started right away.
- Keep your focus on the end product.
- Cut out unproductive work.
- Watch out for things that are stopping you making progress and find ways to overcome these obstacles.

**brilliant** tip

Effective working is smart working. For each part of the task you undertake, this SMART goals mnemonic may help you to remember what you need to keep thinking.

- Specific (What exactly are you trying to achieve?)

- Measurable (What achievable targets can you set yourself?)
- Attainable (What can you really achieve in the time available?)
- Realistic (Is the goal you've set achievable?)
- Tangible (Will you be able to see if you've made progress?)

## brilliant dos and don'ts

### Do

✔ remember you'll need to organise large amounts of information.

✔ keep records of research sources so you can cite them properly.

✔ make sure you adopt a professional approach to presenting data.

✔ allow time for your supervisor to provide feedback and time for you to take it into account and act on it.

✔ set aside time for your dissertation or report to be typed, or, if you need this service, for graphics to be produced or printed, and for the finished dissertation or report to be bound, if that's what your department requires.

### Don't

✘ underestimate how long it may take to do the research or to actually write the dissertation.

✘ start reading aimlessly just to persuade yourself you're doing something.

✘ lose sight of the need to maintain your writing skills at a high level.

✘ plagiarise or infringe copyright. Make it part of your routine to be sure that you don't.

## Don't wait – get started right away

When you know you have to write a dissertation or report, get going as soon as you can. Read a basic text to get some background. Start compiling a personal glossary of specialist terms. Ask your supervisor or tutors questions. Start looking at the current research in your area. Look at online databases to begin your literature search. When you organise your timetable, give yourself a good chunk of time for the initial, general reading to get into the feel of it and make sure you take notes as you go.

> **get going as soon as you can**

### brilliant tip

As you get further into your project you'll find that you think about it a lot. Be prepared to have ideas popping into your head at unlikely times. Carry a small notebook around with you so that you can jot them down. Some may turn out to be bad ideas, but lots could be worth pursuing. Don't just assume you'll remember them. You won't always.

Clear the decks. Finish any outstanding tasks, tidy your work area and let your friends know that you may not be socialising quite as much. (Which doesn't mean you should stop. Keep a balance. Remember, 'all work and no play ...' etc.) Start writing, and that includes note-making, because the act of writing is part of the thinking process. The act of writing isolated paragraphs on the basis of something you've read or an idea you've had can help to clarify your thoughts and they can be the basis for further development once you've read a bit more. And even if you can't use them, just writing out some ideas will help you to go further into the topic and understand it better. The more you write, the more you'll develop your own writing 'voice' and the closer you'll get to your particular take on the topic.

**brilliant** tip

> Many projects stall or get abandoned because the person involved
> is a perfectionist. If you have that tendency, keep telling yourself
> that you may be wasting time trying to get a particular thing right
> when there are lots of other things still to be done. By all means
> get rid of the major flaws but don't get hung up over minor things.
> The important thing is to get the work finished.

Don't let writer's block get in the way. Sometimes the words
flow, sometimes they don't. Just accept it. When you're
finding that putting the sentences and paragraphs together is
a struggle, work through it. Take a break, come back and just
start writing anything, even rubbish. The important thing is not
to use it as an excuse to stop altogether. It's part of the thinking
process.

It won't hurt to review progress each day. Ask yourself:

- What have I achieved?
- What went well?
- What could have gone better?
- Am I keeping up with my timetable?
- What do I need to do next?

## What next?

**You need to make two important lists ...**

... of the things you need to do before you can start properly
and the things you can leave until the project's finished. Then be
strict with yourself. Focus on working through the first list and
don't allow yourself to do anything on the other one – it'll just
be a displacement activity.

## Make an appointment to meet ...

... your supervisor or a potential supervisor. Have a general chat about the whole process, asking what realistic, achievable goals you might set and what they recommend you get started on.

**brilliant** recap

- Be professional in your approach.
- The project may take longer than you expect, so get yourself organised.
- Decide what you'll do, start researching it and thinking about it right away.
- Plan your timetable with care to help you work efficiently and effectively.
- Don't wait, get started immediately. Talk to your supervisor, organise the tasks you need to tackle.

# CHAPTER 2

# Deciding what to write about

Y ou're going to spend some significant time on your research topic, and it's going to occupy lots of your thinking, so you need to choose wisely. It's not just a question of looking through a list of options and deciding 'That doesn't look bad. I'll try that'. There are lots of things to consider – personal, departmental and practical. Let's look at the sort of factors that should influence your choice of topic.

## Weighing your options

The options open to you will depend on your department's policy. In some, your choice may be limited. Rather than asking you what you want to research, the department will give you a list of possible topics. Or there may be a semi-closed list, where members of staff provide suggestions of broad topics but leave you to select a particular area within one or more of them. In both these cases, it may be hard to choose and you may feel it's restrictive, especially if you don't know much about the topics listed. But, in each case, the idea is to give you as much choice as possible in the areas of expertise of the people who'll be supervising and assessing your work. They'll have thought not only about the topics but about practical issues surrounding them and the amount of scope they'll give you for developing your own thoughts on the subject.

If you do have to choose from a list, get moving on it quickly. Some of the topics may be particularly attractive and you'll need to stake your claim early. But don't rush the choice itself. Get all the information you can and allocate time and attention to whatever you need to do to make the right decision. You may want to conduct library or internet searches or discuss aspects of the lists and topics with potential supervisors. Whatever's needed, do it, but get the balance right between a speedy and a considered response.

In some cases, you may not even get a list of options and you'll be expected to choose not only the topic but the specific research question you'll be trying to consider. Your choice may then have to be approved and you may be asked to write an outline of the question, giving a reasoned argument as to why it's worth investigating and describing the way you'll approach it.

### brilliant tip

If you have a specific topic in mind and it's not on a prescribed list of options, try asking a potential supervisor whether it could be considered. But be ready to answer some pretty searching questions about why you think it would make a good research theme.

Whether your system of choosing topics is closed, semi-closed or totally open, there are many things you need to consider to get it right and commit to something that suits you and will produce the best results.

## Making it personal

As we keep saying, you'll be spending a lot of time with this topic so make sure it's something you're interested in, which has scope for exploration and will be a challenge. If you're bored by or indifferent to it, it'll be all too easy to find reasons to avoid it. You need

you need to feel motivated

to feel motivated and use that energy to deal with any problems you encounter.

The fact that you're following a particular course of study indicates that you're already interested in the subject, and your lectures, tutorials and reading will have probably intensified and broadened that interest. But now you're being asked to narrow your focus and look in greater detail and depth at one highly specific aspect of a subject. So how do you weigh up the pluses and minuses of each option? How do you choose?

## Survey the field

If it's an open choice, you could brainstorm possible topics and sub-topics, jot down all the possibilities and rank them in order of interest. Start with broader topics and break them down into more closely defined areas for potential research. Think back on lectures, tutorials, seminars or practicals and the discussions you've had about them. Try to recall which aspects of your course sparked your curiosity and interest the most. Use any criteria you think will help to narrow it down to a favourite or at least a short list.

If you're still finding it difficult to identify a theme that appeals to you, try looking at some of the general periodicals in your subject area – such as *Nature, New Scientist, Time, The Economist* or *The Spectator.* They'll have references to emerging issues, new strands of research or possible controversies arising from contemporary developments in your field.

If you have to choose from a list, look properly at each item on offer. Don't allow knee-jerk reactions to make you reject anything until you know more about it. Read some background information first, and look at some of the recommended texts. Consider all the aspects of each option, then, once again, rank them in order of attractiveness and potential. As before, this should help you to draw up a realistic short list.

A simple way of ranking your choices is to give each one a mark out of ten. When you've looked at all of them, set aside the weaker ones and look again at the ones with the higher marks. Try explaining the reasons for your scores to someone else. Expressing your opinions in words forces you to be clear about them to the other person and, more importantly, to yourself.

## Some other considerations

But, of course, it's not just a question of choosing what you like; you should also think about how useful the experience and the end product might be. In fact, when you've arrived at your short list, giving each topic on it a mark out of ten for usefulness might be one way of ranking them more precisely. It's just one of many practical aspects you need to consider.

> think about how useful the experience and the end product might be

### Possible research approaches

As well as choosing a subject, you need to think about how you'll approach it and what your research angle will be. What sort of challenge does it hold? Will you be answering a question, solving a problem, debating an issue? How broad or narrow will your focus be and how will you control it? What sort of research are you actually thinking of doing? These are all things you should consider. Your answers won't restrict you to a single course of action and your approach may change as you progress, but if you form a detailed notion of your intentions, it'll be easier to make your decision. And having a clear idea of the direction you're taking at the start will enable you to get going quickly and increase your chances of success.

> **brilliant tip**
>
> If you're attracted by a particular research option but are not really sure about how practical or relevant it is, ask around. Talk through its possibilities with a potential supervisor or another member of staff. The more people you discuss it with, the more angles you'll get on it.

## Time

Yes, we're back to time management again. But it's not just a question of organising your schedules; you need to guard against being over-ambitious. One of the questions to ask about your potential topic is: 'Will I have time to do justice to the work and produce a thorough, satisfactory dissertation or report at the end of it?' That will include time to read, analyse and present your material, but also the sometimes surprising amount of time it takes just to get hold of the relevant literature. And there's also the possibility that, if the project is taking up too much of your time, it may have a negative impact on your other coursework.

In some cases, your work may have to be approved by an ethics committee (see Chapter 19). If so, that'll take time, too, and the whole process of actually writing, reviewing and editing a dissertation or a project will probably take longer than you expect. All these considerations should be part of your selection process.

## Getting printed resources

This may seem an obvious thing to say but it's important to make sure you can get the information and material you need to do the work. For example, you'll have to refer to the literature to find the breadth of evidence that'll give your work substance, so you need access to printed material. Find out, therefore, whether you can get access to the books and papers you need:

- in your own institution's library;
- electronically through your library;
- through inter-library loan;
- or by visiting another library.

**brilliant** definition

**Quantitative data**: information that can be expressed in numbers, e.g. the number of patients questioned in a survey.

**Qualitative data**: information that can't be expressed in numbers, e.g. the quality of care provided for patients.

*Getting data*

When you have to collect data and record and interpret your findings, this needs to be factored into your estimate of the time the project will take. If it's quantitative data which you have to analyse, you may have to learn to use a particular statistical analysis software package and that'll take time. If it's qualitative, you need to discuss with your supervisor the most appropriate methods for gathering and interpreting the information. If it involves devising, distributing, collecting and interpreting questionnaires, you'll need to adapt your timing and your techniques accordingly.

## Tracking down sources

Your first stop should be the subject librarians in your library. They'll know most, if not all, of the answers to your questions and will tell you about:

- the resources already in your library, including stored materials;
- the main ways of getting information, including advanced online searches;

- alternative approaches that may not have occurred to you;
- less obvious resources and how to access them;
- contacts at other institutions who can help; and
- exclusive databanks held by professional organisations that you might be able to access through your department.

## How much support and supervision?

You're obviously aware that this is a major undertaking for you, but, even though the work's all yours, you won't be expected to do it entirely on your own. Your supervisor will guide and help you. You'd better find out at the start, though, just how much you can expect from him. Sometimes that may involve regular meetings between you, sometimes you'll only arrange meetings when they're needed. Generally, you'll be able to ask questions, seek guidance and discuss key issues. One area you need to clarify is how far and how often he'll be prepared to review your written work and give you feedback on it. He certainly won't proofread it for you; that's your responsibility. And he may not want to read the whole thing until it's submitted for assessment. So find out these things; it's best to know where you stand right from the beginning.

### brilliant tip

If you have a choice of supervisor, make it someone you feel comfortable talking to, someone who'll give you support and guidance as well as help you to work hard and complete on time. Ask past students how they've got on with different tutors.

## To help you choose ...

Make it an informed choice. Use every available source to explore all the topics you've short listed and the work involved. Discuss them with your course director or assigned supervisor and do some background reading. Make sure you understand all the challenges you may face and, if it seems risky, don't choose it. Speak to students who've already done this kind of study. Get their opinions and reactions about what they felt was important when they were researching and writing it.

**make it an informed choice**

Look at dissertations and reports from previous years. They'll give you an idea of the style and standard that's needed. They'll also help you to appreciate the variety of approaches that may be relevant to your discipline. But don't let their professional structure and appearance put you off. Remember that they were written by students who, at the start, felt much the same as you do now. Learn from them; it'll help you make sure you reach your full potential and produce something that looks, feels and is just as good.

Plan one or more dissertations or reports as part of your decision-making process. Sketch out the overall structure, then think about a more detailed plan. If that's the one you eventually choose, you may not stick rigidly to it but the actual business of writing it will help you to sort out the ideas and decide how appealing and manageable they are.

This is a highly personal and very important decision, so get advice but think for yourself. Try not to be influenced by uninformed opinions or throwaway remarks by others. Some of your fellow students may have their own reasons for liking or disliking certain topics or supervisors. By all means listen to what they say, but use your own judgement, not theirs, when you make your final choice.

## What next?

**The moment you have the necessary information ...**

... choose your topic and be prepared to devote time and attention to it right away. As we've said, you'll need to reflect and dwell on your options but, at the same time, you must be aware that you need to get moving on it or others might get there before you.

## brilliant recap

- Check out the available topics, approaches, options and formats and use them all to make your choice the right one for you.

- Choose early to avoid disappointment and/or having to compromise.

- Organise your time and check the availability of sources of information on your topic.

- Find out how to access those sources and what sort of overall supervision you'll get.

**PART 2**

Getting
organised

**CHAPTER 3**

How to
prepare and
submit a
proposal

Some universities ask you to write a proposal which identifies the topic and the area you wish to investigate and outlines the scope and research methods you intend to use. This is more than an administrative exercise; it'll also help you organise your preliminary thoughts, plan your approach and complete your work on time, so it's worth giving it some close attention.

## What are proposals?

A proposal can have many consequences. Apart from forcing you to look at your aims in a more considered and structured way, it may help the committee assessing it to decide whether it's a reasonable project and who your supervisor will be. It may also be referred to the appropriate ethics committee in your institution. You'll perhaps get feedback on it and advice on how to tackle it.

### brilliant tip

A supervisor may be a lecturer or other member of staff experienced in conducting research and in mentoring students; their input is very valuable. The time they have available for advising dissertation students is precious so it's important to go to all meetings promptly, prepare for them beforehand and communicate effectively when

▶

you do meet. Make a list of questions or issues you want to raise. It'll show your supervisor that you're taking it seriously. And when you get feedback, act on it; it'll almost certainly improve the quality of your work. Remember, too, that your supervisor will be a possible referee when you apply for a job.

## The benefits

A proposal will help you to:

- make sure your aims and objectives are achievable in the time allocated;
- force you to read and review some of the relevant background material;
- check that you're being clear and realistic about possible research methods;
- make you think about what resources you might need at an early stage;
- check that you've considered all the relevant safety and ethical issues that could crop up;
- create an outline structure and a viable timetable for your project;
- find an appropriate supervisor.

### brilliant definition

Hypothesis (plural hypotheses): a theory that can be tested.

## How will it be assessed?

In the simplest terms, the committee considering your proposal will expect you to be able to answer 'yes' to the following questions:

- Do you have an up-to-date and accurate view of the research field?
- Have you outlined the focus of your studies (or the theory you intend to test) in sufficient detail?
- Is the scope of your proposed study realistic in the time allocated?
- Is your proposed research sufficiently original?
- Is it sufficiently challenging?
- Will it allow you to demonstrate your academic ability?
- Will it give you the chance to refine your skills?
- Are the proposed methods appropriate and are you aware of their limitations?
- Are you likely to get access to all the resources you need?
- Are you planning to deal with safety and ethical issues appropriately?
- Are your proposed structure and the underlying research evident?
- Do your proposal's contents conform to departmental or university regulations?
- Have you carried out appropriate background reading?
- Is your dissertation or project report likely to meet the required standard?

Don't try to cover too large a problem or area of discussion. Highlight your central hypothesis or idea and state it very clearly. That means identifying the core of the question or topic that you'll be investigating. You aren't expected to suggest an answer or a conclusion because it's not often possible to do such a thing. The important thing is to consider the evidence from all sides of an argument or case, arrive at a clearly

> don't try to cover too large a problem or area of discussion

stated viewpoint, and give your reasons for it. If your topic adopts an unusual perspective on a research area or focuses on the latest developments in its chosen research field, it may be looked on more favourably.

## brilliant example

Let's assume you're interested in systems of government which have two houses or chambers (i.e. bi-cameral systems). That's too large and vague an area, so you start thinking about how they interact, the checks and balances of such a system, especially when one's elected and the other depends on patronage and selection. This leads you to consider the UK system with its elected and unelected houses and wonder whether that's truly democratic or whether changes might be made to achieve a more equitable balance.

The next step is to explore arguments for and against such changes and consider alternative systems. So the topic that's emerging is a consideration of what method might be used to elect the Members of the Lords rather than accept birth or patronage as qualifications. In order to explore this properly, you'd need to look at the current composition of the Lords and assess how much a selected group of its members participates in and contributes to the governmental process and compare it with the activities of a sample of Members of the Commons.

So, at last, you've dug more deeply and in a more focused way into an area of interest and you can submit a proposal which reads: *Representative Second Chambers: the House of Lords as a case study*.

## What should you write?

Your university may have a special proposal form for you to fill in. If it doesn't, find out what length and structure it recommends, if any, and write a neat, concise outline which you can base on the points listed below. Don't be tempted to try to include too much at this point; there'll be plenty of time to expand it later when you get going on the dissertation/report itself. The members of the committee will have several proposals to consider and they'll need to be able to make a quick decision. If you make yours short and sweet, you'll make their job easier.

### brilliant definition

**Aims**: broad, general statements of overall intent.

**Objectives**: specific, achievable goals which contribute toward realising aims.

## Typical elements of a proposal

It's up to you to decide which of the elements listed on the next page are relevant to your particular field and/or discipline. Some are obvious, others less so, but the list should help you to choose.

Don't rush the preparation of your proposal. If possible, write out a draft and leave it for a few days before coming back to it again to look at it critically and modify it if necessary before handing it in.

> don't rush the preparation of your proposal

Pinpointing a central hypothesis or idea will help you to establish a clear focus, whether you're trying to answer a specific question, investigate a particular issue or highlight a precise topic.

Your proposal's important, but it's only a proposal. You don't need to write the complete work at this stage; the intention is simply to prove that you've chosen a reasonable topic and you're likely to succeed in producing a dissertation or project report that meets your course regulations and requirements.

| Component | Content and aspects to consider |
|---|---|
| Personal details | So that you can be identified and contacted. |
| Details of your degree course or programme | To establish the precise area of study. |
| Proposed title | This should be relatively short; a two-part title style can be useful. |
| Description of the subject area/ summary/background/brief review. Statement of the problem or issue to be addressed | A brief outline that provides context such as: a synopsis of past work; a description of the 'gap' to be filled or new area to be explored; a summary of current ideas and, where relevant, hypotheses. |
| Aim of research | A general description of the overall purpose; a statement of intent. |
| Objectives | A listing of specific things you expect to do to achieve your aim. |
| Literature to be examined | Sources you intend to consult during your research. |
| Research methods or critical approach | How you propose to carry out your investigation. |
| Preliminary bibliography | Details (in the appropriate format) of the key sources you've already consulted. |
| (Special) resources required | All the information sources, samples, instruments, people, etc. necessary to carry out your investigation. |
| Outline plan of the dissertation or project report | An overview consisting of the likely section or chapter headings and subheadings. |
| Names of possible supervisors | This will depend on your university's system. |
| Timetable/plan | A realistic breakdown of the stages of your dissertation, ideally with appropriate milestones. |
| Statement or declaration that you understand and will comply with safety and/or ethical rules | This is the committee's guarantee that you've considered these issues. In certain cases, you may be asked to provide details. |

### brilliant tip

When you write your proposal, it may be the first time you have to think about a title. The two-part style is quite effective, starting with a short, attention-grabbing statement and adding, after a colon or a dash, a longer secondary title that defines the content more closely. You'll have plenty of chances to change it as you work because your research and evolving attitudes may bring out other aspects which take on greater importance.

### brilliant dos and don'ts

#### Do

✔ get feedback from your peers. Show an early draft to a friend or family member, or swap proposals with a classmate. Ask for comments and respond to them. This kind of feedback is especially valuable to make sure that your proposal's logical and easy to follow and understand.

✔ use appropriate language. Your proposal should be clear to the non-specialist, but include subject-specific terminology to show that you understand important concepts and jargon.

✔ set yourself realistic aims and objectives. You need to be original, but you also need to be able to deliver on time.

## What next?

**Imagine you're assessing ...**

... your own proposal. Write a draft and look back at the list of questions we asked earlier. If there are any that you can't reply to with a 'yes', see if you can improve the relevant wording in the proposal or give more evidence to back up your case.

**Make a tentative list ...**

... of possible titles and ask your supervisor or fellow students what they think of them. Look at recent dissertations and project reports to get a feel for the modern style in your discipline.

**Create a detailed timetable ...**

... for your research and writing, including suitable milestones, such as 'finish first draft', and remember to factor in some slippage time.

**brilliant** recap

- A proposal helps you to identify more clearly for yourself and others what you intend to do and how you'll do it.

- Consult the check lists to see the questions it should answer and the elements it should contain.

CHAPTER 4

# Ways to stop wasting time

As a student, you've probably got more freedom than many others to juggle the various needs of study, family, work and social activities but you still need to manage your time with care. The trick is to focus on the right tasks at the right time, work quickly to meet your targets, and make sure you finish everything you start. Time management is a skill; it relies on being organised, setting priorities, and being a good timekeeper. You can learn and adapt it to fit your needs.

> focus on the right tasks at the right time

## Some familiar excuses

Let's start with some 'typical' students and the ways they find to waste time and excuse themselves for it. Do you share any of their attitudes or techniques?

Luke ...

... is a night owl. He likes to work into the small hours. He's got a draft chapter to hand in tomorrow morning, but couldn't face doing it earlier on. Now it's 2 a.m. and he's panicking. The library's shut, so he can't look up a reference he needs. He's tired and he won't have the time or energy to read over his work and correct any errors. In fact, he's so shattered that he'll probably sleep in and miss the deadline altogether. But this is Luke, so he thinks 'Never mind. It's only one chapter. I'll make up the time later'.

## Eleanor ...

... is forever asking her tutor for extensions to deadlines. Her draft submissions are always late but she always finds good reasons for that and it's never her fault. Her tutors aren't amused; they're busy people. If it's not her printer packing up, it's tonsillitis or a visit to Granny in hospital. This time, Granny's ill again; Eleanor's asked for another extension. Her tutor's not amused.

## Lorna ...

... does everything at the last minute. It's only when the pressure's on that she can get going. The adrenaline flows and she produces good work. The trouble this time is that it's her final-year dissertation, all 10,000 words of it. That's a lot of writing, there's only two weeks to do it in, and now she's beginning to get nervous. It's not good for her.

## Ken ...

... has everything under control. No sweat. He reckons the literature he needs to consult is all on the web or in e-journals, so there's no need to panic. He'll catch up on sleep, enjoy his social life and write up his report over the weekend. But there's a problem. His university doesn't subscribe to the journals he'll need, so he'll be able to read the abstracts or summaries but not the full texts. On top of that, the library will be closed at the weekend. Cool or fool? You decide.

## Pat ...

... is a perfectionist. She wants to do really well. She knows the degree she wants and plans to get a great job in her chosen field and start climbing the promotion ladder. She's done very well in her assignments so far and wants the report she's writing to impress, so she's looking for the perfect sentence to start it off with a bang and grab the tutor's attention. But she can't quite get it right. So far she's had fifteen tries at it, but none of them has satisfied her. Time's running out and she's still got the analytical section and conclusion to write. It's not looking good.

**brilliant** tip

Organising your time properly keeps you on schedule, reduces stress and makes deadlines easier to meet. It makes life simpler and increases your confidence. That's especially true for large or long-term tasks because, with them, deadlines seem so far away that it's easy to justify putting things off.

## Diaries, timetables and planners

These stories and their variations are very familiar. They all demonstrate the clear need to get yourself organised and manage your time properly. And the most obvious tool to use is a diary, student planner or wall planner, which is useful for giving you a wide overview of everything you're doing or scheduled to do.

Universities and bookshops sell academic diaries. Like the academic year, they run from September to August. The most obvious use for them and for planners is to keep track of your day-to-day schedules and note when drafts of your dissertation or report are due to be handed in. But you can also use them to work your way back from key dates to create mini deadlines, such as 'finish preliminary reading', 'finish first draft', 'edit first draft'.

Get into the habit of looking at the next day's activities the night before and the next week's work at the end of the week. If you number the weeks, it'll show you how time is progressing (or, more likely, flying). And numbering the weeks in reverse gives you a countdown to important deadlines.

Create a special detailed work timetable. Try to schedule important activities for when you generally feel most alert and energetic. Break the task down into smaller parts and assign to each one the time it needs. If you cross out tasks as you finish them, it'll show the progress you're making.

## Listing and prioritising

At times you may have several different tasks that need to be done. It's easy to forget some, so write them all down in a list each day and decide which should have priority. Number them accordingly, with the most important and/or urgent one first and the least important or urgent one last.

The list will change each day as you work through the tasks. Try to complete as many as possible every day. You'll get great satisfaction out of crossing them off as you do so. If the list has just about disappeared or if all the items have been crossed off, you'll know you've made real progress.

### Important or urgent

Important tasks are those which can be graded by balancing the benefits you'll get from completing them against what you'll lose if they don't get done.

Urgent tasks are those with a time scale.

**brilliant example**

Normally, doing your laundry is neither important nor urgent, but if you start to run out of clean underwear, the situation changes. Priorities don't stay the same. They need to be reassessed frequently.

## Routines and good work habits

Sometimes it helps to do specific tasks at special periods of the day or times of the week. Such routines help with time management. Tuesday morning may be laundry time, Sunday afternoon means a visit to Granny, and so on. You can do the same thing with work-related activities. Set Monday evening aside for library study, for example.

Most of us know instinctively when we're at our best for working. So it should be possible to do important work when you're at your most productive. Save the academic work for when you're 'most awake' and do the routine stuff when you're less alert.

save the academic work for when you're 'most awake'

Some of our time seems like wasted time, such as that spent commuting or just before going to sleep. Use it for thinking, jotting down ideas, editing work or making plans. Keep a notebook with you, even by your bed. You may think you'll remember a great idea in the morning but most people don't.

Organise your documents. If you know where to find things, you won't have to waste time looking.

Often, projects don't go well because they haven't been planned. Working out a detailed plan for a specific project helps you to identify how to structure it. It'll save you time in the long run.

**brilliant** tip

Think about making the working day longer. If you can bear the idea of getting up early, you may find that the extra minutes or hours you get from setting the alarm back a bit are very valuable, especially if it helps you to meet a short-term goal.

## It's hard to start

Procrastination means putting off a task for another occasion. Sometimes it's hard to get started so we invent reasons for leaving things until later. We find something else which we decide is more important or easier, we switch from one task to another, not getting very far with any of them. Or we talk about working, take longer planning it rather than doing it. Perhaps we find some aspect more interesting than others, so we spend too long on that instead of getting on with the rest. And then there's writer's block, which is defined as an inability to structure your thoughts and start writing.

Displacement activities are activities that take the place of others which are more important or urgent. The classic examples are:

● checking and answering texts and emails;
● watching TV programmes or playing computer games;
● spending ages drawing a neat diagram when it's not necessary;
● chatting to friends rather than going to the library;
● shopping, making coffee, making phone calls, tidying your desk, washing the dog;
● convincing yourself that studying in the sun or the pub will work.

Paradoxically, planning can also be a displacement activity. We keep stressing the need to plan, but it's possible to do too much.

If you're planning all the time and not actually getting anything done, the balance is wrong. What's happening with all this is that your subconscious is telling you you're actually busy when, in fact, you're just avoiding doing things. So you need to make a conscious effort to overcome it. Think about what you're doing.

Set yourself times or targets and reward yourself for meeting them. You could decide, for example, to write 500 words or the next part of your chapter and then give yourself a break.

> set yourself times or targets and reward yourself for meeting them

Use the list tactic to write down all the things you have to do and label them as 'immediate', 'soon' and 'later'. Then don't look at the 'soon' and 'later' categories until you've crossed off all the 'immediates'. And don't think that concentrating on the smaller things will free up your mind for the bigger things; you'll just find other smaller things to take their place.

## It's hard to finish

Delaying finishing a piece of work is also procrastination. It's a particular problem for perfectionists. If you understand the importance of time management, you'll know that it's wasteful to keep trying to make something perfect before submitting it. The satisfaction and achievement of finishing several tasks competently are greater than those of perfecting just one.

So what can we do to stop procrastinating and start managing our time better?

## brilliant dos and don'ts

### Do

✔ improve your study environment. Tidying up can be a form of procrastination but if you create a tidy workplace from the start, it makes studying easier and there are fewer distractions. Cut down on noise; it's usually other people's noise that interrupts your train of thought so consider studying in a quiet place like a library. Or indeed find a location where there won't be any interruptions and, to make sure your focus is entirely on the work to be done, only take with you the books and papers you need for it.

✔ work in short bursts when you're concentrating well, then give yourself a brief break and start again.

✔ find a way to get started that suits you. Students sometimes worry too much over finding an impressive, high-impact opening sentence. There's nothing wrong with starting with a simple definition or restating the issue or problem. If you just can't get going, think of the bigger picture – your degree, your career – and see the task to be done as a small but important part of the journey.

✔ cut large tasks up into manageable, achievable chunks. You'll feel better if you have a small task ahead rather than a massive one. And try to get one or more of these chunks finished every day. Completing lots of little jobs is easier than completing one huge one and, in the end, they come to the same thing.

✔ try working alongside others (unless you've opted for a quiet, solitary study location). It's comforting to have people doing the same sorts of things and you can cheer each other up, encourage each other and even stop for a chat over a drink or coffee after each study period.

### Don't

✘ let yourself be distracted. Learn to say 'No' (politely) to friends. Hang up a 'do not disturb' sign and tell them why. Work somewhere else and don't tell them where to find you. Switch off your phone, TV or email program.

✗ be negative. If you get anxious about how your task may be received or assessed, you'll find it harder to get going. Don't let those negative things interfere. Focus on the things you do know, not those you don't. You have no idea how the task will be seen or received so don't waste nervous energy speculating about it. Remember your good results.

✗ always start at the beginning of a written task and work through. With word-processing you can work out of sequence. So, if you're writing a long report, it might help to start with a more 'mechanical' part of it, such as a reference list or results section. You could also write out the summary, abstract or contents list. That'll get you going and also give you a plan to work to.

✗ be afraid to ask for help. If you feel that you don't know enough about, for example, maths, spelling, or how to use a software program, don't let it hold you back. Fellow students, lecturers, skills advisers, websites – there's help all around you.

✗ try to make everything perfect. This is all about managing time. It's precious and we must give each task its fair share. Perfection is very hard work and the nearer you get to it, the more time and energy it takes to achieve minor improvements. Use the time on the next task instead.

## Serious time management

How do you really use your time? It's a difficult question to answer. So it might be an idea to keep a detailed record of what you do for a few days. You can make fancy spreadsheets and work out percentages if you like (as long as you're not doing so as a displacement activity). Whatever method you use, it'll help you see the things that are simply time-wasting and cut back on them. Check the amounts of time you spend on useful activities, too, and get the balance right between them.

## Create artificial deadlines

- Set a finishing date earlier than the official submission deadline for your dissertation or report and stick to it. That'll give you time for the important process of reviewing your work, correcting errors and improving its presentation.

- Always expect the unexpected. If a timetable's got no flexibility, it won't be able to accommodate such things. So build in some gaps. Be flexible.

- It may be that you're committed to a single activity which takes up the bulk of your time – an outside job, socialising, looking after a partner or family member. If that's the case, you probably need to make some changes because you must find room for your studies. If you're uncertain where to start, make an appointment with a student counsellor.

- And, at a mundane but still important level, get the tools to help you manage your time – a diary, wall planner, personal digital assistant (PDA), mobile phone with diary facility, alarm clock. And don't just leave them lying in the drawer – use them.

# What next?

**Experiment with ...**

... listing and prioritising. If you haven't used the technique before, test it out for a week or so. Write down all your current and future tasks, assignments, appointments and social events. If they're big, break them down into smaller tasks. Number and rearrange them in order of priority. Then work your way down the list. After the test you'll know whether it worked for you or not. Did it make you more efficient? Did things get done on time?

## Declutter and reorganise ...

... your life. Start with your room and study environment. Tidy things away and only leave out what's needed for current activities. It'll all help to make life much easier and less stressful.

**brilliant** recap

- Good time management is essential; our examples show how typical excuses and displacement activities waste precious work time.

- Use diaries, timetables and planners to organise your time for both short- and long-term tasks.

- List and prioritise individual tasks according to their importance and/or urgency. Keep the lists updated and develop good routines and work habits.

- Getting started may be hard, but don't put it off.

- Use these dos and don'ts to help you organise your work and time efficiently.

**CHAPTER 5**

# Dissertation planning

I n broad terms, your dissertation will show your abilities in two main areas. First of all, you'll have to show that you know and understand the general topic and can research a specific aspect of it, thinking critically about the information, views and conclusions of others. You'll then need to organise your material and support your arguments with relevant evidence in a well-structured text that follows the appropriate academic conventions. In other words, you must control with care what goes into your dissertation and how it's organised.

## Creating a plan

If there were a 'one size fits all' plan, we'd describe it but, unfortunately, there's not. People think and write differently and any particular approach may suit some but not others. Some plan meticulously, others simply sketch a bare outline. Too much detail can prevent ideas expanding, too little may leave gaps. The ideal is a plan which is devised specifically for the project in hand and has just enough detail to lead you through the argument with confidence and still enough flexibility for you to adapt it as you write.

### Establish the main themes

You've written a proposal, discussed the topic with your supervisor, so your ideas about it have already started to take shape. What you need to do now is deepen your understanding of them

deepen your understanding by reading the relevant literature

by reading the relevant literature. This'll reinforce your own thinking and probably reveal differing viewpoints and arguments for you to consider. All the material you collect – both for and against your own view – will help you to present a tight, well-argued case and reach a balanced conclusion.

So it's not enough just to list facts, and that's where your choice of plan comes in. You want to present the evidence for and against in a logical, structured framework that best supports your own response.

## Realistic time planning

Yes, we're back to time management again; it's fundamental to good planning. When you know the submission date, you'll be able to work out how much time you have available for the various phases of your work – research, first draft, further reading, editing, proofreading and anything else that occurs.

### brilliant tip

Good initial planning is invaluable. Breaking the project down into smaller, separate tasks will save time and make the whole thing less stressful. Getting yourself properly organised at this early stage will free you to focus more directly on each task as it comes along. You'll always know where you are.

So look at the course regulations to get your submission date. Work out how long you have between now and then and how much of that time you can devote to doing the work. Remember that there'll be other calls on your time, such as lectures, tutorials, practicals and part-time work commitments. Factor all those in and divide the time that's left into convenient working periods, allocating realistic periods to each aspect of the task.

Your list might look something like this:

- Working out how you'll approach the topic
- Preliminary reading
- Planning the overall structure
- Supplementary reading
- Writing the first draft
- Reviewing the first draft
- Rewriting as necessary
- Editing
- Proofreading
- Printing/writing out the final copy
- Time to allow for the unexpected

Beside each element, write how long you think it might take and set a date for it.

## Exploring the topic

So, to begin with, you need to analyse the topic and try to establish exactly how you'll approach it. If you've written a proposal, start with that and develop the various aspects you've mentioned. If not, try creating a brainstorm map by just jotting down anything that occurs to you which may be relevant to the subject. The idea is to fix some initial personal thoughts before you're influenced by any reading material. Take as wide a view as possible of the broad area you intend to work on, or, if you've already decided on a title, refine and deepen what you think it means. This is where your critical thinking skills come in as you analyse the topic, decide what's important about it and why. Once you start reading and researching, you'll be able to add to and refine the map as your knowledge and understanding grow.

**brilliant tip**

To create an effective brainstorm map, use a single sheet of A4 in the landscape position. This gives more space for lateral thinking and creativity. It also leaves space for adding more ideas later.

## Finding and selecting relevant source material

However confident you are, it'll still be useful to get some general background information about the topic. You may or may not be given a reading list. If you are, you'll probably find that it's quite extensive to give you some choice. It'll have basic texts and then sources that go into greater depth. It may also be quite long, but don't imagine that you have to read everything on it. In some subjects, you may need to look at just one or two recommended texts, but whatever its length or apparent complexity, approach it systematically and you'll find it very rewarding. But remember, it's only a start; you're writing a dissertation, so you'll need to go beyond it and find other sources for your particular topic.

*Where to look*

- The library is an obvious starting point. You can use the electronic catalogue to find books and/or articles on your topic. It's also useful to look at the shelves devoted to the subject you're researching. You may come across titles which weren't suggested as fitting your search words but which may be relevant. The reader's adviser or liaison librarian can advise you on specialist material and sources specific to your field of study.

- Handouts and/or PowerPoint slides often outline key issues and ideas, and identify problems and possible solutions.

- If you've been conscientious about noting the lecturer, topic and date of lectures, it'll be easy to find lecture notes which are relevant to your topic.

- General or subject encyclopaedias are good for giving a thumbnail sketch of useful background information and they usually refer you to more detailed texts. Electronic versions may be available through your university library.

- E-book facility Ebrary is a reliable resource which is easy to consult and use.

- E-journals contain specialist material which is reliable and probably the most up-to-date writing on your topic.

When you're researching, time is precious, so it makes sense to be as efficient as possible in identifying the material you need. Use the contents page and index of books to find which sections are relevant to your topic. Some authors put key pages in bold type in the index and this helps you to focus your reading rather than look up every single mention.

Make sure right from the start that your reading and note-making are focused. As you move from general texts to more specialised ones, you'll collect facts, examples, information to support a particular viewpoint, arguments opposing it. You'll be deepening your understanding of the topic and building up a more informed picture of events, implications of a procedure or possible solutions to a problem. You can add them all to your original brainstorm map.

**brilliant tip**

If you're stuck, try asking the basic questions which trainee journalists are advised to use:

Who's involved? What are the problems/issues? When, where, why and how did it all (or will it all) happen?

## The basic possible structures

All this reading will generate lots and lots of ideas. The secret is to know what to keep and what to discard. This is where you

**the secret is to know what to keep and what to discard**

need to be really disciplined in your appraisal of the material you've gathered. Try asking these questions to help you sort out what's important to your study:

- Who are the key actors in a sequence of events or decisions?
- What criteria can you use to explain particular situations?
- What explanations support a particular view?
- Can you identify any patterns in the material?
- Are the processes governed by things such as short-, medium- or long-term factors?
- What common or isolated themes have you noted in different treatments of the same issue?

Once you've analysed the material in this way, you should be in a position to decide how best to structure your approach and argument. It may best be suited by one of the commonly used models: chronological, classification, common denominator, phased, analytical, thematic, comparative/contrastive. We'll outline these in a moment but, before you choose, try to stay flexible. What you want is something that'll help you to create an organised, logical, coherent argument and you may find that what works best is a combination of these methods or 'nesting' one inside another for one or more segments of your study.

### Chronological
This is a description of a process or sequence, such as outlining the historical development of the European Union. It's a kind of writing that's most likely going to be entirely descriptive.

### Classification
Classification means putting objects or ideas in order. Let's say your topic is transport and you're examining ways of travelling by land, sea and air. That already gives you three classifications

and each can be sub-divided into commercial, military and personal modes of transport. You could then sub-divide even further by considering, for example, how they're powered. To some extent, how you divide and sub-divide is subjective, but the approach does give you the chance to describe each category at each level in a way that allows some contrast. It's particularly useful in scientific disciplines and any context that lends itself to starting with the general and moving on to the more specific.

## Common denominator

This lends itself to topics where there's a common character-istic or theme. If, for example, you're investigating levels of high infant mortality in developing countries, the implication is that there's something missing in these different countries which results in children dying. So the common denominator is deficiency or lack. Your plan might, therefore, group its material under the following headings:

- Lack of primary health care
- Lack of health education
- Lack of literacy

## Phased

The phased model is for when you're identifying short-, medium- and long-term aspects of an issue. A study of the impact of water shortage on flora and fauna along river banks could look at:

- short-term factors – the river bed dries out in the summer and so annual plants die;
- medium-term factors – oxygenating plant life is damaged and wildlife numbers fall;
- long-term factors – the water table gets lower and lower and certain amphibious species decline.

*Analytical*

Analysis means examining an issue in depth and it's used to consider complex issues. Suppose you were evaluating potential solutions to the problem of identity theft. Your approach might follow an outline plan like this.

● Define identity theft, and give an example.

● Explain why it's difficult to control.

● Outline legal and practical solutions to the problem.

● Weigh up the advantages and disadvantages of each.

● Say which ones you would favour and why.

**brilliant tip**

Analysis is useful for many kinds of dissertations and reports. It's also helpful when you're having trouble identifying themes or trends. There's a method called the SPSER model which helps you to break topics down into their components. SPSER stands for Situation, Problem, Solution, Evaluation, Recommendation. It works as follows:

● Situation: describe the context and give a brief history.

● Problem: describe or define the problem.

● Solution: describe and explain the possible solution(s).

● Evaluation: identify the positive and negative features of each solution and give evidence and/or reasons to support your viewpoint.

● Recommendation: identify the best option in your opinion and say how you came to your conclusion. (You can leave this element out, depending on whether you're asked to provide a recommendation or not.)

## Thematic

This is similar to the phased approach, but in this case the identifying characteristics are not sequences but themes. Each topic will produce its own themes but possible examples could be:

● social, economic or political factors;

● age, income and health considerations;

● gas, electricity, oil, water and wind power.

## Comparative/contrastive

Comparing and contrasting derives from the themed approach. Let's take as an example a study which involves considering arguments for and against the introduction of car-free city centres. That's a perfect opportunity for using a grid-style way of organising notes into positive and negative aspects for the main interested parties in the debate.

|  | Positive aspects (P) | Negative aspects (N) |
|---|---|---|
| 1 Pedestrians | Greater safety, clean | Lengthy walk, poor parking |
| 2 Drivers | Less stress; park and ride facilities | High parking fees; expensive public transport |
| 3 Commercial enterprises | Quicker access for deliveries | Loss of trade to more accessible out-of-town shopping centres |
| 4 Local authority | Reduces emissions | Cost of park and ride |
| 5 Police | Easier to police | Reliance on foot patrols |

Interestingly, you can structure your dissertation in two different ways using this plan. The introduction and conclusion will be similar in each case, but the way of constructing the main body will be different.

1  After the introduction, move vertically down the 'positive' column. Now do the same with the 'negative' column, then write a short conclusion to establish the balance between

them. (So the main body sequence is: P1, P2, P3, P4, P5, N1, N2, N3, N4, N5.)

2  After the introduction, look at pedestrians and examine the positive and then the negative aspects for them. Now do the same with each of the other categories of people, then write your conclusion. (The main body sequence this time is P1, N1, P2, N2, P3, N3, P4, N4, P5, N5.)

## Expanding your outline

The outline plan is the basis for what you write. Follow it through, making sure you don't miss out any points. Check, too, that the links between sections that you noted in the plan are clear in the text so that the reader is led logically through your argument.

### *Explain your approach*

The models we've described are fairly standard and easily recognisable approaches to academic writing assignments, but it's still important to tell your reader early on, usually in your introduction, which one you intend to use.

## What next?

**Look at a chapter in a basic textbook ...**

... and analyse the structural approach the author has taken. Note how much space she gives to 'scene-setting' using description and to the other components of the text, such as analysis, argument and evaluation.

**Take some dissertations ...**

... or past exam papers, find the ones that have been framed as questions and try to work out which structural model they've followed, either overall or in each part.

## brilliant recap

- A plan is a framework which helps you to structure your main themes. Link it closely with your working timetable.

- Explore the topic, decide why it's important and start choosing relevant source material.

- Choose an appropriate structure from the seven basic approaches to written assignments.

- Taking time with your plan will make the dissertation easier to write.

**CHAPTER 6**

# Planning your experimental project

We've already stressed the need for good time management and, with experimental project work so central to many science degrees, it's important for you to make the most of your time and effort in the lab or field. That's what this chapter aims to help you do.

## The value of organisation

In science, good observation and experimentation are essential. You're trained to create hypotheses, design experiments, gather and analyse data, present results, and draw conclusions – all essential and useful skills which a research project helps you to develop. And, even if you don't intend to be a researcher when you graduate, this experience will give you a good insight into how science works and the principles of good scientific practice.

good observation and experimentation are essential

Most science degrees involve project work and give it a significant weighting when it comes to assessing your achievements – maybe up to 25 per cent of your final grade. So if it's that important, it makes sense to put time and effort into producing a piece of work that'll earn you a good mark.

**brilliant** tip

Most project work is scheduled for your final year. By then you'll know what topic you want to study in depth, and you'll have developed the knowledge and skills to handle it effectively. In some courses, though, you may have to do short projects earlier in your course to help you start acquiring the necessary skills and experience. Whether your present task is one of these smaller projects or your honours submission, treat it seriously.

## Be organised but flexible

Once you've decided on your topic, your supervisor will probably help you to identify a starting point for your research – it might be a 'simple' set of observations, an uncomplicated experiment, or a test of a key instrument or technique. But as you start investigating the subject, keep an open mind and be prepared for your own ideas to change. Your research may uncover different areas of interest, so you need to be adaptable in your planning. If the results you were expecting don't materialise, don't be afraid to change tactics and use different methods, conditions or experimental subjects.

A good supervisor will help you to interpret results and modify your initial plan if necessary. Remember, though, she's probably quite busy herself, so ask for advice from other people in her team. The important thing is to keep making progress; if something crops up which is holding up your work, don't just accept it, get help to solve the problem.

Being aware of and describing the various stages of your research may well be an important part of your eventual report because it'll show how you've applied the scientific method. You'll get credit for:

- assessing and interpreting your results logically;
- designing your experiments to take account of them;
- drawing conclusions based on all the evidence.

## brilliant tip

Don't be upset if you get so-called 'negative results'. They're a vital part of scientific progress and your personal development as a scientist, so turn them to your advantage; explain what happened and why and, if you can, alter the design of your next experiment accordingly.

## Know where you're going

If you're going to plan your thesis, report or dissertation effectively, you need to have a clear idea of what you're expected to submit right from the start. You'll be able to make better plans, gather the right information, analyse your data appropriately and think about ways of presenting your results. So, before you get into your research:

- Check your course handbook or regulations to find out about things such as how long it's supposed to be, how it should look, what the learning objectives and marking criteria are, and when it's due to be handed in. Knowing that date will help you to plan the various phases properly.

- Look at project reports by past students. You may find them in your supervisor's lab or get them from the students themselves. They'll give you a good idea of the style, content and quality of presentation that's expected.

- Talk to staff and postgraduate students. They may be able to give you extra information and advice about your subject.

## brilliant definition

**Thesis (plural theses)** – a (substantial) written paper or report on a specific topic. It's frequently used to describe an honours project report.

## Draw up a schedule

You'll probably have at least one term or semester to complete your project and, at the start, that may give you the feeling that there's plenty of time to think about what to do and how to do it. But that's deceptive. Lab and fieldwork are time-consuming and you'll have only a few limited sessions in which to get everything done, perhaps just one or two a week. On top of that, it's unusual for research to go completely smoothly; something always seems to crop up. So students often find they're having to rush their project at the end, which isn't a good idea. It'll affect the quality of your write-up, and may eat into energy and time you should be spending on other things, such as final exams. So what you need is a plan of action which takes account of the various phases you'll need to negotiate.

> what you need is a plan of action

### *Preparation*

Reading, surveying, ordering equipment or chemicals, making up solutions – all these, and the many other things you need to get yourself going, take up time. Make a list of what you have to do and get it done as quickly as possible.

There may be preliminary observations or experiments for you to do in preparation for later work or as part of your dissertation or project. If you do a 'quick and dirty' experiment, it'll let you practise your technique and maybe reveal flaws in your approach.

### 💎 **brilliant** definition

**Confounding variables** – Whenever you alter a particular variable in an experiment (for example, the pH, or acidity, of a bathing medium for cells) you'll also alter other things. These are confounding variables. If you have controls which alter the confounding variable but not the original one, you can test which variable actually caused the results you've observed.

## Testing and writing up your central hypothesis

This will call for a set of observations or experiments which will form the core of your report. Again, don't expect them to run smoothly; you may get interrupted, or some tests may have to be repeated, and you should always be ready to move to 'plan B'. Make sure your experiments include suitable controls for all confounding variables.

You'll need time to analyse and present your data. It can be a drawn-out process and the best idea is to do it as you go along. That way, if your analysis reveals anything that needs you to change your approach, you can do it before you're too far into the project.

## brilliant tip

No experiment is perfect. But you need results to present and discuss so it's better to get some from an imperfect design rather than wait until you can do the best experiment possible. Even if things don't turn out as you hope or expect, you can still earn marks by pointing out the flaws in your own work. Remember, we learn by our mistakes.

The writing-up and proofreading part always takes much longer than you think so, again, try to write up as much as you can as you go along. For example, there's no reason why you shouldn't write a draft introduction very early on. Also, if you write up the materials and methods section while you're working, you're less likely to forget or make a mistake about the details. And it's essential to leave plenty of time for editing and proofreading.

---

### ✖ **brilliant** dos and don'ts

**Do**

✔ create and prioritise a daily checklist of things you intend to do, then do them.

✔ any background work that'll help you to get on more quickly, and read about any techniques or equipment you'll be using so that they'll be familiar to you.

✔ lay out tables in your lab notebook ready to receive results.

✔ bring the right equipment and clothing, and make sure, if you need to discuss results with your supervisor, that your graphs and tables meet the necessary standards, and that you know what they show and where you're going next.

✔ get your workspace ready for the next day's tasks.

**Don't**

✖ get distracted by others who are working to a different timetable.

✖ leave your bench space, fume hood or cupboard in a mess. Label specimens or solutions and store them appropriately.

---

## Recording information and results as you go along

If you keep all results and information up to date you'll save yourself lots of time. Put all the details of what you're doing in a lab notebook and copy down lab schedules and protocols that apply to your work. If you leave this until later, you may take ages finding them.

The same applies to your observations, experiments and data analysis. Use any spare time to create good, accurate graphs and jot down notes for your results and discussions sections.

We've already suggested writing a draft introduction early on. Every project report needs one and your supervisor can probably suggest a few research papers or reviews which relate to your particular project. You can start from there and expand your knowledge of the relevant literature.

**brilliant** tip

Citing and listing references is often a tedious, time-consuming and even confusing task. You can make it faster and easier by finding out the formatting style your discipline or department prefers and using it to record the details for each reference in a word-processed file as you go along. If you leave it and try to deal with all the references at the same time, it'll take you much longer. Of course, there are software packages for creating reference lists, but it takes time to learn how to use them.

## Take a professional approach

- Stay safe.
  By the time you reach the stage of carrying out a project of your own, you'll have had lots of lab safety training. There are rules and guidelines to protect you, but you're also responsible for your own safety and the safety of those working around you.

- Think ahead.
  Good preparation saves time. Always be on the lookout for ways to get ahead of the game, such as booking a key instrument, and stay aware of all the different needs that may arise.

- Write up as you go along.
  We keep on emphasising this because it's important. Experimental work often involves periods of waiting. Don't

waste them, use them to get on with some of the mundane tasks of writing up.

- Communicate with your supervisor.
Be ready to show him any preliminary results and discuss them with him. It'll help you to think about what the results mean and could make the next phase of your work easier to organise. If things seem to be going wrong, discuss this as soon as possible so that you can fix them.

- Back up your files.
Every aspect of the project takes lots of your time and effort so it would be frustrating if you lost any of your hard-earned data or notes. On top of that, the project mark is vital to your degree classification so it's just common sense to keep back-ups of all your files.

- Leave plenty of spare time near the deadline.
Despite all the dire warnings they get from supervisors, students nearly always underestimate how long it'll take them to write up the final report. It needs care and attention and lots of thought. And there's always the possibility that something unexpected, such as a printer malfunction, may happen. So plan to leave yourself as much time as possible near the submission date.

## What next?

**Look in your ...**

... course handbook or regulations to find the format you're supposed to use for your report. It'll help you to draw up an appropriate plan of action. You'll find the typical layout of a standard experimental research project report in Chapter 21.

**Create appropriate filing systems ...**

... for your experimental project work. You'll need files for hard-copy resources, such as methods protocols and safety sheets, electronic files for the word-processed parts of your report and, if necessary, spreadsheet-based data collection and analysis. Get them ready at the start and you can add and organise material as you go along.

**Discuss your plans ...**

... with others. They can offer valuable advice that'll help you create successful plans and adapt to any setbacks. Don't work in isolation; compare notes regularly with your fellow students and involve other lab workers and your supervisor wherever possible.

**brilliant** recap

- Good scientific practice needs you to be organised but flexible. Be systematic but keep an open mind.

- Talk to others and check past examples and course regulations to make sure you're doing the right things.

- Draw up a plan of action which includes time to prepare and conduct experiments and test and write up your hypothesis.

- Organise information and results as you go along and be professional.

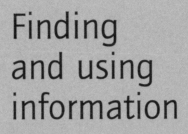

**PART 3**

# Finding
# and using
# information

**CHAPTER 7**

# Information
# literacy

When you start your dissertation or project, your supervisor will probably suggest a few things for you to look at to get you going but it's your project, so you'll be expected to source most of the material for yourself. That means exploring resources specific to your area of research by getting to know more about your university library. You'll have used it already in your studies but now you'll be looking from the viewpoint of a researcher and it's that perspective we'll look at in this chapter.

## Using the library

Modern university libraries are more than just places where books, journals and archived material are stored, they're information centres that offer electronic gateways to a massive amount of online information. To access all that efficiently, you need to develop skills which are part of what's sometimes called 'information literacy'. They're skills which are essential to your research studies and they may take you into areas and facilities that you haven't seen or used before. In fact, you may find that tracing the detailed material you need is quite challenging.

> develop ... 'information literacy'

## The basic skills

You've no doubt used the library quite a bit in your studies so far so you'll be familiar with how the system works. You'll know:

- how to use the electronic catalogue for your own and other libraries;
- where to find books by using one of the two common cataloguing systems;
- how to find a periodical or journal in hard copy or e-journal format;
- the rules about borrowing, including how long you can keep the material you've borrowed and the fines you'll have to pay if you don't return them on time.

If you're not sure about any of these things, ask about them right away.

In case you hadn't noticed it, this is the electronic age and things change fast. Library information systems aren't static. Institutions subscribe to new or different suppliers of online information through various media, especially e-journals. You'll probably find that your library provides an online information portal dedicated to your subject area, but it's best to contact the librarian responsible for managing these discipline-specific resources right at the start to make sure you're on the right track and that you haven't missed some vital link. Find out who she is, tell her what you're researching, and ask her to suggest where you should start looking.

## brilliant tip

As well as contacting the librarian with responsibility for your discipline, check to see whether there are any training sessions on how to use referencing packages or new or subject-specific databases. Look at the library's website, too, for tips on accessing online databases and e-journals. And don't forget to look at any hard-copy library leaflets with guidelines about using their facilities and resources.

## The different types of source material

You'll be working your way through a lot of material, some from primary, some from secondary sources. These terms can mean slightly different things depending on your discipline and Chapter 9 deals with this in more detail, but it's worth identifying some of the basics which you may find useful.

- **Monographs** are books on a single, often quite narrow subject.

- **Reference works**, such as encyclopaedias, year books and dictionaries, carry facts and definitions and give you a quick overview of a subject. You'll find them in the area of the library reserved for reference material. You can't usually borrow them.

- **Research papers** are very detailed 'articles' published in journals, covering specific subject areas. They can also be proceedings of conferences where delegates have presented papers on cutting-edge research.

- **Reviews** offer analyses of a particular research area which are often very detailed and more up to date than books.

- **Textbooks** are useful for giving you an overview of your field of study.

- **Websites** published by official bodies should give you information you can rely on, but be careful – others aren't so reliable. They may be useful for comparing viewpoints and sourcing other information but you should use them with care.

One important point to note about using sources is that you should consult a number of different ones on any particular topic. They may reinforce or contradict one another, offer varying views or support different interpretations. The process is known as 'reading round' your subject and by exposing yourself to different opinions in this way, you'll be in a better position to analyse ideas and you'll demonstrate to the marker that your research has been thorough. It's part of the all-important skill of critical thinking.

## brilliant tip

A quick way of getting started or checking a point is to use one of the main search engines. Within fractions of a second you'll get pages and pages of links, some of which will be very useful. But you need to be very careful and make sure that the sites you're looking at are authoritative sources and that the information they're offering is correct and can be backed up. If the material seems to be useful, try checking it against references from recognised academic publications, online or in hard copy.

### E-resources

Libraries have subscriptions to e-book repositories, e-journals, e-newspapers and online dictionaries and encyclopaedias. Your own institution will have its dedicated system of letting you access these digitised and web-based resources, usually through the library's website. Some are open-access, but for others you'll need a password. You'll normally need to log on to a university network computer to initiate an ATHENS username and password. Different institutions have slightly different systems so it'll pay you to get to know the details of yours as early as possible. Just ask a member of the library staff.

They're not only useful resources, they're also available 24/7 from any computer connected to the internet. They may also allow more than one person to access an e-book at the same time and some e-book facilities, such as ebrary, have extra tools which let you search, make notes and consult linked online dictionaries to check the meanings of words. But it's important to remember that copying and/or printing out from such sources is covered by copyright laws.

## brilliant tip

Get your ATHENS password through your institution's library as soon as you can. ATHENS opens a gateway to many different databases used by academic researchers. Your password will identify you as an authorised user for as long as you're a student.

## Important techniques for online research

It's probably already obvious to you that the type of research you'll be doing for your dissertation or project is deeper than anything you've done before in your studies. The reason for this is that you must base what you write on reliable, refereed evidence that's comprehensive and up to date. Giving just a few isolated references you found through internet searches or Wikipedia won't work. You have to identify and access new sources and there are three main ways of doing so:

1  **Database searches** find sources based on keywords related to your research topic. What you get from them is a list of reference details and an abstract or summary of material from a wide range of sources. You can then look through the list and choose any that look useful. Of course, you can't be sure they're what you want until you've read the full paper, but this technique helps you to focus on specific aspects of your topic.

2  For **citation-based searches** you start with a particular article and its list of references and work back through the sources the writer himself has used. Go through the list,

picking out and looking at any books or articles which seem relevant. You can go further back if you want by looking at the sources cited in their lists too. What you'll get from this is a broader 'feel' for the literature of your subject area. Remember, though, you're working backwards so that won't uncover any sources that are more recent than the article you started with.

3  **Searches using citation indices** let you work the other way, i.e. forward in time. You need access to databases such as the *Science Citation Index* or *British Humanities Index* which give details of publications that have cited a given reference. So you start with the reference and, by seeing who's cited it, you work forward in time towards research that's been published after it appeared. It's a useful tool if you're working with slightly dated sources.

You may not be able to access some of these sources because they may have appeared in journals to which your library doesn't subscribe. If you really think something's worth following up, though, you may be able to get the article through inter-library loans. There's a specialist inter-library loan librarian who'll be able to help you with this but it's not a free service and you'll probably have to pay for it yourself.

## Other libraries and other resources

Most libraries share resources with those of neighbouring institutions and they're all linked to the UK's national library, the British Library. This receives a copy of every publication produced in the UK and Ireland. It holds over 150 million items and 3 million more are added each year. Some university libraries hold key documents of the European Union; they're designated as European Documentation Centres (http://ec.europa.eu/europedirect/visit_us/edc/index_en.htm).

There are now several electronic databases which make it easier to get access to information from public bodies, and most of them are available online. For example, you can look at statistical population details on the National Statistics website (www.statistics.gov.uk), and any papers and publications produced by the Houses of Parliament at www.parliament.uk. Access to academic journals and other material will depend on whether your library subscribes to them or not, so find out which search engines and databases are available to you.

**brilliant** tip

The web's always changing, growing, adding more and more information. Material appears and disappears very quickly. That's why it's vital to keep a detailed record of every reference you find online, and note the date when you last accessed it. If you don't, you may not be able to find it again.

## Organising your resources and notes

Dissertation or project research can generate lots of material, from your own notes to hard copy, printouts, photocopies and material you've read online. So, with all this material to organise, you have three basic problems:

> dissertation or project research can generate lots of material

1 how to file and organise the hard copies;
2 how to cross-reference your notes so that you get the right references in the right places;
3 how to create a database which makes it easier for you to create a list of all the references you cite.

### *Hard copy*

Perhaps the simplest, 'low-tech' way to store hard copy and the reference information about it is to create a record card for each item. Give each document a number in sequence (1, 2, 3 …) and store them in boxes or files in the same sequence. For each one, create a card with the same number and on it write all the essential information about author, publication, date and so on, together with any comments you want to make about the item itself.

Store the cards in alphabetical order by author. Then, if you want to refer to something in an article written by E. Burke (2003), you can find the 'Burke' card, note the number on it and use that to locate the relevant article in your file or box. It takes time to create and maintain the system and it means you'll have to type up the final reference list as a single exercise, but you might prefer it to the computer-based and database models below.

### Personalised computer-based approaches

You can use the same numbering approach for a computer-based system. Create a folder with sub-folders devoted to different themes or aspects of your work. In each sub-folder put a word processor file of a simple table listing the sources in numerical order along with the usual detailed references for each one and your own notes about the content and its relevance to your study. If you prefer, you could use a spreadsheet instead of a Word table. You can add any material you like to items in the folder, such as direct quotes from sources, downloaded materials, and pieces of ongoing written work. It's then easy to create your reference list by cutting and pasting the relevant details into a separate file and sorting them alphabetically.

There's one issue to consider when using either of these methods, though. You'll need to devote time to doing some serious cross-checking and proofreading of the final list to make sure that all the conventions of the referencing method are applied consistently.

## Using commercial bibliographic software

Our third suggestion is to use one of the many versions of commercial bibliographic database software, such as *EndNote*, *Reference Manager* or *ProCite*. They do make it relatively easy to organise citations in your text and prepare your reference list. What you need to do is enter the appropriate bibliographic data into fields in a database. Some versions actually help you to search online databases and upload the data from them. You can then search the database and customise it in a style you prefer to create a consistent reference list.

The advantage here is that the system will avoid any inaccuracies in punctuation in the final version. In addition, most of these packages let you insert citations according to different referencing methods and alter their output to suit different publication requirements. The downside, though, is that your project may not have all that many references and it's debatable whether it's worth spending valuable time learning how to use whichever package is available to you.

**brilliant dos and don'ts**

### Do

✔ register for any courses introducing new information-handling packages. Librarians often run specific training sessions to introduce more complex information management software. They'll take up some time but may be well worth it.

✔ take advantage of reciprocal library arrangements. Your university library may have agreements with others in your area, including national libraries, and you may be able to borrow books from them too.

✔ join the local authority library. It may hold material you won't find in the university library and you may find that the demand for a particular book is lower there than in the university library. You might also be allowed to borrow it for longer.

✔ define your catalogue and database searches carefully. Surnames, for example, are often spelt in different ways – Brown/Browne, Nichol/Nicol/Nicoll. If you can't find a work by an author whose name you haven't seen in print, try different spellings. Remember, too, that English pronunciation can be very different from how a word is spelt – St. John ('*Sinjun*'), Mainwaring ('*Mannering*') or Marjoribanks ('*Marchbanks*'). If you're having problems searching a database, especially if you're looking for something that's crucial for your study, ask a subject librarian for help. He may be able to use advanced methods or resources that you don't know about.

✔ keep your cross-referencing system as simple as you can. There's no 'one size fits all' technique; it depends on your personal preferences, the type of research you're doing, the subject area, and other factors. It may be satisfying to create a fully functional database or a beautifully colour-coded cross-referencing system but don't forget you're working to a schedule and time is precious.

## What next?

**Get to know ...**

... the electronic library resources available to you. Look, in particular, at any subject-specific resources listed in the catalogue system or on the library website.

**Explore the shelves ...**

... covering your subject area. Use the library catalogue and the information in the shelving aisles to find where it is and browse the shelves. This often reveals interesting resources which you might not have found otherwise.

**Find out about ...**

... alternative library facilities. That might mean satellite libraries on different campuses or in different buildings or departmental libraries with specialist resources. They may have duplicate holdings of books in the main library. You may also find them more suited to the way you like to study, even if they don't cover your subject area.

**brilliant** recap

- Use libraries and their different types of source material efficiently and effectively.

- Identify e-resources and expand your online research.

- Organise your resources and notes and make it easy to access them, using hard copy, computer files or bibliographic software packages.

# CHAPTER 8

# Learning how to read

Whatever you're studying, it's sure to involve lots of reading. There may be bits you can skim through and there'll definitely be bits you need to linger over to deepen your knowledge and understanding. In this chapter we'll look at some skills which will help you to read more efficiently.

## Reading and understanding

Most of the books and chapters you'll be reading as part of your research will be written in a fairly formal, traditional academic style. Sometimes that can mean they look and feel like heavy going. Big, unfamiliar words, long sentences, an apparent lack of passion – all these things can make reading feel like hard work. But these materials have been written by people who want to communicate information and/or a point of view, so they're carefully organised to make their points. If you learn how text is structured, you can use that knowledge to help you read it in a way that'll make it understandable and yet save you time. That's what we mean by reading more efficiently.

**brilliant** tip

Most of the time when you're reading source materials, you'll be taking notes. It's possible to do both at the same time, but that may not work well because your notes could end up just being

▶

a rewrite of the text. If you scan the relevant section of text first, it'll give you a clearer idea of its content and how it fits into the argument and you'll be able to write more meaningful (and probably much shorter) notes.

## The overall organisation of the text

You'll be dealing with different sorts of texts. They may be recommended by your supervisor or perhaps books and articles you find for yourself when you're expanding your reading. Whatever the source material, the best strategy is to do a quick survey (not a read) to get an overall idea of what's in it. There are various ways of doing this.

> the best strategy is to do a quick survey

- Does the title sound as though it'll be about the things you're looking for?
- Is the author a well-known authority on the subject?
- Does the 'blurb' on the cover confirm that it's relevant to your needs?
- When was the book published? Will you get up-to-date information from it?
- Look at the list of contents. Do they cover the topic areas you need? Are the chapter titles very general or quite detailed?
- Is there a comprehensive index and is it easy to use? Take a quick look for specific references to the material you want.
- And finally, what does the text look like? Is it easy to read, easy to navigate using sub-headings?

These are your starting points. Once you've worked through this list you'll have a better idea of whether that particular piece is valuable for you. It may be that you decide you need to read the whole book, or there may just be certain chapters or pages that cover what you're looking for. Equally, you may decide that there's nothing there you need at present.

## Why are you reading?

This may seem a strange question but it's part of what you need to do to help focus your reading. Before you start the actual reading, make up your mind exactly what it is you're looking for and adapt your approach accordingly.

## brilliant questions and answers

**Q** Are you looking for a specific piece of information?

**A** If so, use chapter titles, subheadings or the index as a guide and read only the relevant pages. It'll speed up the whole process.

**Q** Are you reading in order to appreciate the author's style or the aesthetics of perhaps a poem or a work of fiction?

**A** If so, you'll read more slowly, taking time to reflect on the choice of words and expressions and you may reread certain parts.

## The structures of academic writing

Academic texts usually follow the same basic pattern. Each part of the argument, as well as the overall piece, consists of an introduction, the main body of the text and a conclusion. Both the introduction and the conclusion may consist of one paragraph or several. Each paragraph, including those in the main body of the text, has its own particular point to make or develop and each starts with what's called a topic sentence which indicates what the paragraph contains.

**brilliant** example

The typical layout for a piece of work consisting of five paragraphs looks like this:

Introduction (Topic paragraph)
Main body (Paragraphs 2, 3 and 4, each beginning with a topic sentence)
Conclusion (Terminator paragraph)

The way these paragraphs and the sentences within them fit into the overall argument is usually signalled by 'signpost words'. They guide the reader through the logical structure of the text. For example, the word 'however' warns you to expect that whatever follows it will contrast or conflict with whatever went before it, and if you see 'thus', you'll know that you're about to read a consequence of what went before because it means 'as a result of this'. So look out for signpost words; they'll help you to identify general meanings, changes of direction and the underlying argument.

A quick way of getting a general overview of the text is to read topic and terminator paragraphs, or even just their topic sentences. Unfortunately, that won't be sufficient to supply your needs, but it'll get you focused on what you're likely to gain from your reading of the whole piece.

**read topic and terminator paragraphs**

Another useful technique is to scan quickly through the text for keywords related to your interest. You may notice that several occur in particular paragraphs, which suggests that those paragraphs are worth reading in detail. If there are headings and sub-headings, they'll be very helpful in the same way.

## brilliant tip

We're looking at the structures of texts in order to help you to decode them as a reader. It's as well to remember that, if you want to make your own work easier to decode (by a marker, for example), you should use the same layouts and techniques. For both reader and writer, the better the material is structured, the more effective it is at conveying information.

## brilliant example

Here's a more detailed example of a piece of writing with the structural features we've been talking about highlighted for you. We've put the topic sentences in italics and the signpost words in bold.

(INTRODUCTION, OR TOPIC PARAGRAPH)

*Technological advances and skilful marketing have meant that the mobile phone has moved from being simply an accessory to a status as an essential piece of equipment.* From teenagers to grandmothers, the nation has taken to the mobile phone as a constant link for business and social purposes. As a phenomenon, the ascendency of the mobile phone, in a multitude of ways, has had a critical impact on the way people organise their lives.

(BODY TEXT)

***Clearly***, *the convenience of the mobile is attractive.* It is constantly available to receive or send calls. While these are not cheap, the less expensive text-message alternative provides a similar 'constant contact' facility. At a personal and social level, this brings peace of mind to parents because teenagers can locate them and be located by them at the press of a button. **However**, in business terms, while it means that employees are constantly accessible and, with more sophisticated models, can access internet communications also, there is no escape from the workplace.

▶

*The emergence of abbreviated text-message language has wrought a change in everyday print.* **For example**, pupils and students have been known to submit written work using text-message symbols and language. Some have declared this to mark the demise of standard English. **Furthermore**, the accessibility of the mobile phone has become a problem in colleges and universities where it has been known for students in examinations to use the texting facility to obtain information required.

*The ubiquity of the mobile phone has generated changes in the way that services are offered.* **For instance**, this means that trains, buses and restaurants have declared 'silent zones' where the mobile is not permitted in order to give others a rest from the 'I'm on the train' style of mobile phone conversation.

*While the marked increase in mobile phone sales indicates that many in the population have embraced this technology,* **by contrast,** *'mobile' culture has not been without its critics.* Real concerns have been expressed about the potential dangers that can be encountered through mobile phone use.

*One such danger is that associated with driving while speaking on a mobile.* A body of case law has been accumulated to support the introduction of new legislation outlawing the use of hand-held mobile phones by drivers whilst driving. The enforcement of this legislation is virtually impossible to police and, **thus**, much is down to the common sense and responsibility of drivers. **Again**, technology has risen to meet the contingency with the development of 'hands-free' phones which can be used while driving and without infringing the law.

*A further danger is an unseen one, namely, the impact of the radiation from mobile phones on the human brain.* Research is not well advanced in this area and data related to specific absorption rates (SARs) from the use of mobile phones and its effect on brain tissue is not yet available for evaluation. **Nevertheless**, although this lack of evidence is acknowledged by mobile phone companies, they advise that hands-free devices reduce the SARs levels by 98%.

*Mobile phone controversy is not confined only to the potential dangers related to the units alone; some people have serious concerns about the impact mobile phone masts have on the area surrounding them.* The fear is that radiation from masts could induce serious illness amongst those living near such masts. **While** evidence refuting or supporting this view remains inconclusive, there appears to be much more justification for concern about emissions from television transmitters and national-grid pylons which emit far higher levels of electro-magnetic radiation. **Yet,** little correlation appears to have been made between this fundamental of electrical engineering and the technology of telecommunications.

(CONCLUSION, OR TERMINATOR PARAGRAPH)

*In summary, although it appears that there are enormous benefits to mobile phone users, it is clear that there are many unanswered questions about the impact of their use on individuals.* At one level, these represent an intrusion on personal privacy whether as a user or as a bystander obliged to listen to multiple one-sided conversations in public places. **More significantly**, there is the potential for unseen damage to the health of individual users as they clamp their mobiles to their ears. **Whereas** the individual has a choice to use or not to use a mobile phone, people have fewer choices in relation to exposure to dangerous emissions from masts. **While** the output from phone masts is worthy of further investigation, it is in the more general context of emissions from electro-magnetic masts of all types that serious research needs to be developed.

## Speed-reading

The basic techniques of speed-reading were developed in the 1950s by Evelyn Wood, an American educator. She set up institutes to teach students skills which enabled them to read hundreds of words a minute. Her methods have been used in many fields where busy people need to read and understand lengthy papers as quickly as possible.

*The techniques*

People who read quickly don't read each word as a separate unit. They use their peripheral vision which, if you stare straight ahead, is what you see at the edges of your vision to the right and the left. By doing this, they take in groups of words at a time. So, instead of reading:

Students need to read many books in the course of studying,

they read:

(Students need) (to read many books) (in the course of) (studying.)

In other words, rather than moving their eyes 11 times, once for each word, they move them 4 times. It's obviously a more efficient and less tiring way of reading. Studies have also shown that people who read slowly are less likely to gather information quickly enough for the brain to understand it, so reading slowly may actually make comprehension more difficult.

You've already done plenty of reading as you've studied and you're probably a skilled reader but, before we go any further, maybe you'd like to check your reading speed (although not if you're just using it as a displacement activity). There are two possible methods: one measures how much you can read in a given time, the other how long it takes you to read a specified amount of text.

In method A you'll read for a particular length of time.

- Choose a chapter from a textbook. Don't use a newspaper or journal because the text there is often printed in columns.
- Calculate the average number of words to a line, e.g. if there are 50 words in five lines, that's ten words per line.
- Now count the number of lines per page. Let's say it's 41.

- Multiply the number of words per line by the number of pages – that's 10 × 41 = 410 words on each page.

- Start at the beginning of your chosen text and read for a set period of time – let's say 4 minutes – without stopping. Note the point on the page at which the time runs out.

- Let's assume that you managed 2½ pages in 4 minutes. To find out how many words that is, multiply 410 (the number of words per page) by 2.5 (the number of pages you read). That gives you 1025 total words read.

- Now divide that by 4 (the number of minutes you read) and it shows that you've averaged 256 words per minute (wpm).

Method B uses a text of a known length.

- Choose a text and count the number of words in it. Let's say it's 744.

- Time how long you take to read it. We'll say 170 seconds.

- To find how many minutes that is in decimal form, divide it by 60, which gives you 2.8.

- Now divide the total words by 2.8 and you get a reading speed of 266 wpm.

Since you're a student and you do quite a bit of reading, you probably already use a version of fast reading to some extent but there are ways of improving your technique.

*Eye gymnastics*

Here's an exercise which helps to train your eyes to use your peripheral vision when you're reading. As you do it, your eyes will be forced to jump from one group of words to the next, focusing on the centre each time. Try to read the text quite quickly from left to right in the normal way. If you feel some discomfort behind your eyes, it means they're adjusting to this new way of moving. Just keep practising. You can use this text as a piece of training equipment just as you'd use a treadmill or a barbell.

| | | |
|---|---|---|
| Learning to read quickly | is a skill | that needs to be developed. |
| If you have to read | a new piece of text | you will find it useful |
| first of all | to read | the first paragraph |
| and the last paragraph | of the text. | From this |
| you should be able | to gauge | the context |
| and general outline | of the relevant topic. | While it is true |
| that all academic texts | should be fully edited | before publication, |
| it does not follow | that every text | follows these conventions. |
| However, | a well-written piece | of academic writing |
| should follow this pattern | and, as a reader, | you should exploit |
| this convention | in order to help you | to understand |
| the overall context | before you embark | on intensive reading |
| of the text. | | |

| | | |
|---|---|---|
| When you are about to | take notes from texts | you should not begin |
| by sitting | with notepad ready | and the pen poised. |
| Certainly | make a note of | publication details needed |
| for your bibliography, | but don't try | to start taking notes |
| at the same time as | beginning | your first reading. |
| It is better | to read first, | reflect, recall |
| and then write notes | based on | what you remember. |
| This gives you | a framework | around which |
| you ought to be able | to organise your notes | after you have read |
| the text intensively. | People who start | by writing notes |
| as soon as | they open the book | will end up |
| copying | more and more | as they get more tired. |
| In this case | very little | reflection or learning |
| is achieved. | | |

## Finger tracing

Another technique is finger tracing. As its name suggests, it's when you run your finger along under the line of text you're reading. It follows the path of your eyes across the page, starting and stopping a word or two from either side. This keeps your mind focused on what you're actually reading and stops you skipping back to previous sentences or jumping forward to the text that follows, and it helps to increase your eye speed. Some people use a bookmark or ruler held just under the line they're reading; it's a useful guide and works in the same way.

Try this exercise:

- Choose a reading passage about two pages long. Note your starting and finishing time and calculate your reading speed using method B.

- Take a break of 40–60 minutes then go back to the text and run your finger along the lines much faster than you could possibly read it.

- Now do the same thing again but slowly enough for you to be just able to read it. Note how long it takes you this time and work out your wpm again. You'll probably find that you're faster this time round.

- Now do the same exercise at the same time of day over a week, using texts of the same sort of length and complexity.

*Speeding up and slowing down*

The average reading speed is around 265 wpm but various factors may make that slightly slower for university students. Texts may be more difficult, their terminology unfamiliar, and they may be discussing quite complex concepts which need to be absorbed. All these things can slow down a reading. But the more familiar you become with your subjects and the issues being covered in your course, the faster you'll be able to read.

As well as trying to get faster, you should think too about things that might slow you down. They could include:

- distractions such as background noise, TV, music, talking;

- sounding each word as you read it aloud;

- reading word by word;

- being over-tired;

- poor eyesight – your eyes are too important to neglect, so get them tested; reading glasses can make a big difference to your studying comfort as well as to your speed reading;

- poor lighting – if you can, read using a lamp that can shine directly on to the text; reading in poor light causes eye strain, which makes it harder to concentrate and cuts down your reading time.

## Other strategies

- Skimming.
  Let your eye run quickly down a list or over a page looking for a key word or phrase, just as you do when looking for a name in a phone book. That's the way to find a specific piece of information you're looking for.

- Scanning.
  Let your eye run quickly over a chapter this time. It'll give you an idea of what the chapter's about before you start.

- Picking out the topic sentences.
  Read the topic sentences to add more detail to the overview you got from scanning. It'll help you to understand what's being conveyed before you study-read the whole text.

- Identifying the signpost words.
  They'll guide you through the logical process mapped out by the author.

- Recognising clusters of words which go together grammatically.
  As you read, group words in clusters according to their natural sense. It's what you did in the eye gymnastics exercise and it'll help you to make fewer eye movements.

- Taking cues from punctuation.
  Full stops, commas and the other punctuation marks are valuable clues when it comes to understanding a text. They separate chunks of meaning, indicate points to emphasise, mark transition points and help comprehension in many other ways. As reader and writer, you should never underestimate the importance of punctuation.

## Speed with comprehension

Measuring speed on its own gives a false result. It's all very well having a wpm of 300 or whatever but if you don't understand what you're reading, you're wasting your time. So speed reading needs to be matched by a good level of comprehension. There are ways of testing your understanding to make sure you've grasped the main points of what you've been reading. The one we'll look at is called the SQ3R method, which stands for Survey, Question, Read, Recall and Review. It's also useful when you're revising for exams because it helps to develop memory and learning skills simultaneously.

survey, question, read, recall and review

With the SQ3R method, you can't just read on autopilot and not retain much, you have to process the material as you go along. Let's go through the five stages: S, Q, R, R, R.

### Survey

● Read the first paragraph (topic paragraph) and last paragraph (terminator paragraph) of a chapter or page of notes.

● Read the topic sentences of all the paragraphs between them.

● If there are headings and sub-headings, focus on them.

● Study graphs and diagrams for important features.

### Question

● What do you already know about this topic?

● What's the author likely to tell you?

● What specifically do you need to find out?

### Read

● Read the entire section quickly to get the gist of it, using finger tracing if it helps.

- Go back to the question stage. Check and revise if necessary the answers you gave then.
- Look for key words, key statements, signpost words.
- Don't stop to look up unknown words – get it read.

*Recall*

- Turn the book or your notes over and try to remember as much as possible.
- Make important pattern headings/notes/diagrams/flow charts.
- Look at the text again and see how accurate your recall was. Do this after every 20 minutes of reading.

*Review*

- Take a break, then try to recall the main points.

## Reading effectively and with understanding

After everything we've said, it must be obvious that reading isn't the simple process that most people assume it to be. You need strategies and practice to make it work for you. So start by thinking about why you're reading. Look at the material you've already collected, such as lecture notes, which can remind you of how a topic was presented, what arguments were used or how a procedure was followed. Decide whether you're trying to get a general overview or identify additional specific information.

And when you've decided that, use a technique and material that suit your needs and a reading speed that fits the type of text you've chosen. For example, an interesting article in a newspaper won't demand much in the way of intensive reading whereas an important chapter in an academic book will.

Get the general message before focusing on the difficult bits. Not all texts are reader friendly. If you come across a section of text that's difficult to understand, skip over it. Forcing yourself to read and reread it won't make it any clearer. Read on and then, when you come to a natural break in the text – the end of a chapter or section – go back to the hard bit and try again. It'll probably make more sense now because you've got a better feel for the context. The same advice applies to new or difficult words. Don't stop every time you come across one; read on and try to get an idea of what it might mean from the rest of the text. You can look it up when you've finished and add it to your personal glossary.

Follow up references in your text. Be aware of any citations to other authors you find there. They won't all be relevant to the aim of your reading, but it's worth making a quick note of any that look interesting as you come across them. You'll usually find the full publication details at the end of the chapter, article or book and you can use them to find and read them when you've finished the current text.

**brilliant** tip

Take regular breaks. If you try to read continuously over a long period of time you'll retain less. You can concentrate well for 20 minutes and more but, after 40 minutes, the mind begins to wander. Take plenty of rests (but make sure they don't start getting longer than the actual studying periods).

## What next?

### Check your reading speed ...

... using the two methods we've described. If you think it's slow, try out some of the techniques and exercises we've outlined. Decide which ones suit you, use them for a while, then check to see if your speed's improved.

**Practise surveying a text ...**

... using a book from your reading list. Rather than simply opening it at a particular page, spend 5 or 10 minutes surveying the whole book. Think about how the author has organised the content and why. Remember this as you read the text, and reflect on whether it's helped you to understand and absorb the content more easily.

**Remember that ...**

... grammar, punctuation and spelling provide useful clues to meaning. Look for these visual cues and use them to help both your speed and comprehension.

**brilliant** recap

- Make your reading more efficient by surveying a text's overall organisation before you read it more closely.

- Ask why you're reading a text and adjust your technique accordingly.

- Study these explanations and examples of how sentences, paragraphs and the writing itself are structured.

- Use speed-reading techniques, strategies and exercises but make sure you don't sacrifice understanding.

**CHAPTER 9**

# Assessing the value of source material

Nowadays, we have access to more information than we can handle. It's important, especially for those involved as teachers or learners, to evaluate evidence, data and opinions with great care. That's why we're now going to look at where information and ideas come from, how to check whether sources are reliable, and the differences between fact, opinion and truth.

## How to filter and select reliable material for discussion

Whatever the subject of your dissertation or report, you've got to be able to evaluate information and ideas. It's a skill which has many forms and applications and which will differ according to the task in hand. You may be analysing information to test its truth or accuracy, the reliability or potential bias of the person or organisation that produced it. Or you may be evaluating it in relation to some argument or case. You may also come across evidence which contradicts it or may even find conflicting arguments which are based on the same information. It's a complex process and it'll be up to you to sort out the conclusions to which the bulk of the evidence leads. So let's look first at where ideas and information come from and what they actually are.

## Information and ideas

Facts and ideas come from someone's research or scholarship. They might be descriptions, concepts, interpretations or numerical data. And you only know of their existence because they're out there in the public domain, which means that they've been communicated or published. The place in which they first appear is called the primary literature. If they're modified and reappear, they do so in what's known as the secondary literature. You need to understand and know this when you're doing your own analysis and evaluation of information and deciding how to cite evidence or references in your own work.

facts and ideas come
from someone's research
or scholarship

## Checking 'facts'

Not all 'facts' are true; they could be misquoted, misrepresented, frankly untrue or based on a false assumption. That's why you need to be so careful with lots of web-based information because you can't know whether it's been properly tested or edited. So, if misquotation and misinterpretations are so frequent, it's logical to say that the closer you can get to the primary source, the more likely you are to be nearer the truth of what was actually said or written. Mind you, you then have to ask who wrote it and who paid them to do so. That's why an important element in assessing sources is to investigate the ownership and 'provenance' of the work. In other words, find out who wrote it and where and why they did so.

### *The author*

So who wrote it? If it is signed or there's a 'byline' identifying the author, you can check his credentials to decide whether his ideas can be trusted. If he turns out to be an authority in the area, the decision's easy. If you're not sure about him, a bit of research, such as typing his name into a search engine, might help. Mind you, just because he's Professor Such-and-such, it doesn't mean what he writes is definitely true. But if you know he's someone whose opinions on the subject are based on years of research and experience, you'd probably stick with him rather than quote some anonymous author on a website. And if the source you're reading doesn't identify the author, it could mean either that he's not willing to take responsibility for the content or that there's a reason for him to hide.

*Provenance*

Provenance means 'where did it come from?' If the author's place of work is mentioned it could tell you whether there's likely to have been any academic study behind what he's written. If he works for some public organisation, he may have to follow particular rules of publication and perhaps have his work checked over by a committee before it's published or distributed. Authors in that sort of set-up are more likely to get into trouble if their material turns out to be scurrilous or incorrect. And if he's writing for a company, a political party or some other vested interest, how much pressure might have been put on him to bend the facts to suit their message?

**brilliant tip**

In most published academic sources, author and provenance are easy to find. The information may even be printed just below the title. With the web, though, it's a different story. But you can check the information in the header, body and footer of the document for clues.

## The nature of evaluation

In 'scientific' subjects you'll need to interpret and check the reliability of data before you can set up and test meaningful hypotheses, so evidence-based evaluation is an essential skill which underpins the whole scientific approach.

In 'non-scientific' subjects, ideas and concepts are important but they need to be supported. So you may need to carry out an objective analysis of information and arguments in order to build your own position and back it up with evidence.

## Facts, opinions, truth

As you're researching your dissertation or report, you'll read plenty of books and articles and come across lots of varying viewpoints, so it would be all too easy to get confused and mix up fact, opinion and truth. In many fields, such as arts and social sciences, there's often no 'right' or 'wrong' answer. Instead what you get is a range of stances or viewpoints, but as long as you construct your own argument and support it with evidence, you'll get credit for it. The easy option is to follow the party line and regurgitate what you've heard in lectures or read in a textbook but it's more productive (and more interesting) to follow your own path. Even if your supervisor doesn't share your conclusions, she'll mark your work according to the way you've presented it.

In some subjects, such as history, politics and economics, it's easy to stray into opinionated and biased conclusions; they may even be value judgements. If you submit viewpoints such as these, without reliable evidence to support their accuracy and relevance, you may be marked down.

Discussing the nature of truth could lead us into deep waters and philosophical confusion. We don't need to go into the murky world of politics (the word 'murky' makes that a value judgement, by the way) to know that truth has many faces and that 'factual' statistics can prove opposing things. In discussion and debate, you can only agree that something is true when all sides of the argument accept it. If you can show that a particular line of argument lacks credibility or is unacceptable in some other way, it'll strengthen the arguments against it.

Of course, the central features of this question are the notions of objectivity and subjectivity. Objective judgements are those based on a balanced consideration of the facts, whereas subjective judgements are based on the opinion of the individual making them. In the academic world, the preference is for detached, objective writing. But that doesn't mean you can't have opinions. On the contrary, you'll be encouraged to form your own views on the issues in your study. The key is to produce valid reasons for them.

> the central features are the notions of objectivity and subjectivity

## How reliable is your information?

We'll explain and give examples of terms such as 'logical fallacy', 'propaganda' and 'bias' in Chapter 14. They're all part of the problem of this potential confusion of facts, opinions and truth, so we're offering some checklists which will help you to decide whether the information you're getting is reliable. The more satisfactory and positive the answers you can give to their questions, the more reliable you can assume the source to be.

*Authorship and the nature of the source*

● What's the author's name?
● What qualifications does she hold?
● Who employs her?
● Who paid her to do the work?
● Is this a primary or a secondary source?
● Has it been refereed or edited?
● Is the content original or derived?
● Does the source cite relevant literature?
● Have you checked a range of sources?

*The information and its analysis*

- Is the source cited by others?
- Is when the source was written important with regard to the accuracy of the information? For example, was it written at the time the events occurred or later and therefore with hindsight?
- Have you focused on the substance of the information presented rather than its packaging?
- Is the information fact or opinion?
- Are there any logical fallacies in the arguments?
- Does the language used indicate anything about the status of the information?
- Could there be any numerical errors?
- Are the statistics used to analyse the data appropriate?
- If there are graphs, are they constructed fairly?

## The provisional nature of information

Some things which were once considered incontrovertible facts now seem ridiculous. Centuries ago, they thought the Sun orbited the Earth (and their observations even seemed to confirm it). On the other hand, there are things which seemed absurd, such as the idea that continents could float and drift, which are now accepted as facts. There are also massive changes in social 'truths' which, over a long period, can alter the whole framework and terminology of discussion. Any debate on slavery, for example, or the emancipation of women would now be very different from its counterpart a couple of hundred years ago. This is why the academic world encourages challenges to accepted fact and opinion. An open and enquiring mind is an asset as long as it supports its views with sound, up-to-date reference points.

## Presenting and supporting your argument

● Your dissertation or report will probably be assessed on how convincing your argument is and how well you use the evidence to support it. So what is this 'evidence' we keep mentioning? Well, it comes in many forms, from statistical/numeric sources through quotations to direct observation. Wherever you got it, ask yourself if it's relevant and valuable. And always note where you got it in your own writing. If you don't, the marker may recognise it as someone else's idea and you'll get no credit for it. You may also be accused of plagiarism.

● Don't just highlight your side of the argument; try to produce a balanced conclusion. Be open about counter-evidence that doesn't seem to support your case. Explain what others of a different persuasion think or might think, then say why you've arrived at your own conclusion. This is all part of the critical thinking process.

● If you're not certain about something, cross-reference it by looking at several sources and comparing what they say. Make them as independent as possible. There's little point in comparing an original source with one based directly on it. If you find the different sources agree, it may make you feel more confident of your position; if they don't, you may need to decide which viewpoint is the more persuasive.

● How old is the source? 'Old' doesn't necessarily mean 'wrong', but ideas and facts may have altered between when it was written and now. Can you trace changes through time by comparing the sources you have? Are there any important events, works or changes in methods which may influence conclusions?

● Look at the range and quality of citations provided by the author. They may show how much research she carried out beforehand and prove that her ideas or results are based on genuine scholarship. If you're not sure how good the work is, have a look at some of these references. Are they up to date? Do they refer to independent work, or is she mainly quoting herself or one particular researcher?

- Look beneath the surface – at substance rather than presentation. Just because information is in a glossy magazine or on some well-constructed website, it doesn't necessarily mean it's reliable.

- Analyse the language she uses. Is it subjective or objective? Personal opinion or objective conclusion? Are there any signs of propaganda or bias in expressions such as 'everyone knows ...', 'I can guarantee that ...'? Does she distort the evidence to suit her case, or use exaggeration, ambiguity, journalese or slang? Your analysis will help you to evaluate the quality and probable reliability of her work.

- However reliable it seems to be, it's probably a good idea to be a little sceptical about the facts or ideas involved and question the logic of arguments. Even information from primary sources may not be perfect; at the time it was written a particular approach may have seemed legitimate but may no longer apply or may lead to different conclusions. If you're finding the viewpoint very attractive, try not to identify too strongly with it. You need to stay detached when you're assessing its merits and flaws.

- Look for fallacious arguments and logical flaws. Analyse the method being used to convey the facts rather than the facts themselves.

## What next?

### Analyse the nature of your sources ...

... each time you come across something which seems to be relevant for you. Decide whether the sources on it are primary or secondary, and why. If they're secondary, do they quote any of the primary sources? Try to get a copy of one of the primary sources and check whether it might have been modified on its way to the secondary source.

## brilliant recap

- Access and evaluate information and ideas, using primary and secondary sources.
- Establish the accuracy of 'facts' and distinguish between opinions and truth.
- Be sure that the information you find is reliable.
- Use the checklist to help you to research and present a balanced argument.

**CHAPTER 10**

# Turning reading into notes

M ost dissertations and projects have recommended reading lists. They'll probably include textbooks, journal articles and web-based materials. Sometimes you'll get specific references to topics covered in these texts but at other times it'll be up to you to find material for yourself. The reading technique we discussed earlier will help you to pinpoint the parts of the text that are relevant and, in this chapter, we'll look at the various note-making techniques you can use.

## The need for notes

You've probably already done lots of note-making but dissertations and reports are larger projects and may call for a different strategy. You need ways to compress information into a form that captures the important points and makes them easy to access and understand later. The way you organise your notes can also help you to plan the structure of your work.

### brilliant tip

Develop good habits and you'll save lots of time both with note-making and consulting the notes later. So right from the start, remember two techniques:

● Before you do anything else, make a note of the full details of the source. That means the author's name and initials, the title,

▶

the publisher and the date and place it was published. Don't forget to add the chapter and pages these notes refer to.

● Make your notes personal by using underlining, highlighting, colour coding, numbered lists, bullet points, mnemonics or anything else that helps you to find your way around them. Choose a distinctive layout with maybe boxes for important points. If you're consistent with this, it'll make the different aspects of your notes instantly recognisable.

## What should be in them?

With some texts, you'll just be looking for a few specific points but others will need to be read more fully and more closely. The first thing for you to decide is why you're actually making the notes. There are many possible reasons. You may want to:

● create an overview of the subject;

● record a sequence or process;

● analyse a problem;

● isolate the logical steps of an argument;

● compare different viewpoints;

● borrow quotes to support a point you're making;

● add your own ideas to the text or comment on the points it's making.

As you can see, each of these is asking a different question and the style, detail and depth of your notes will alter according to their purpose.

Often, the tendency is to start with a sheet of paper in front of you and a pen clutched in your hand. You open the book, start reading and begin jotting down 'important' points as you go along. The trouble with that is you end up writing out whole chunks of the text and it doesn't encourage you to think much about what you're reading; it goes from the page to your notebook without dwelling long in your head. So, once you've decided why you're making notes, get used to following a routine:

● Decide what style and layout are best for the particular task you're doing.

● Scan the section you'll be reading.

● Establish what the writer's trying to do. Is it a narrative of events or a process, a statement of facts, an explanation, a presentation of a logical argument, an analysis of a problem, a critique of an argument?

● Work out his approach and viewpoint and decide how they relate to what you're looking for.

Then, as you're making your notes, jot down ideas of your own which may be triggered by the text and highlight any links you see with other texts and lectures.

> jot down ideas of your own and highlight any links with other texts and lectures

Finally, don't just copy the author's words, use your own. It's his meaning you want, not his words. But if you do want to copy something directly from the text, put it in quote marks and note carefully the page on which you found it.

## Note-making formats

When you're researching a dissertation or project, pressures of time and perhaps limited access to books and articles mean that you have to be really accurate with your notes. You'll also need to order them in a way that helps you to remember their context and significance.

When you think about making notes, it's perhaps automatic to assume that you start on line one and jot things down as you work through the text. This is fine, but there are different formats for different purposes. If you wanted, for example, to stress the two sides of a particular argument, it might be more helpful to have two columns side by side, one carrying points for, the other points against. Or if you were brainstorming and just writing down disparate ideas, they wouldn't necessarily follow a connected, linear sequence. In that case, it might make sense to use what's called a mind-map or spider diagram, where you write them down as they occur, placing them near ones which are similar or in a separate area and using lines to connect notes that may belong together.

> there are different formats for different purposes

In fact, we can identify seven basic note-making formats, although there are variations on all of them.

### Keyword notes

This is a fairly obvious and common format. Topics are identified by a keyword which is jotted down on the left, maybe in the margin. Then all points relating to that topic are written opposite it. It means that you can quickly find a specific part of the argument and all its aspects are gathered conveniently together. But it does depend on the source text having a systematic structure. If it doesn't, you may find you've moved on to other topics and then there's a reference back to a previous one, so you have to jump back in your notes, you might lose the thread of your reading, there may not be enough space left on the page, and so on.

### Linear notes

Another obvious format. Once again, it helps if the text is presented logically. This time, instead of keywords, you use numbers. But not just 1, 2, 3 and so on. Think of 1 as a keyword and 1.1, 1.2, 1.3, 1.4 as the various points relating to it. Again, it's a good way to gather and organise material but, as before, if you come across something that you want to add under an earlier number, it may be hard to find room for it in the sequence.

## Time lines

This has limited use as a format. It consists of setting a time line on the left and noting events or the stages in a process opposite the appropriate times and/or dates. Once again, it's difficult to go back and insert material at an earlier time. On the other hand, it does give a strong visual aid if the object of the note-making is to remember sequences.

## Flow charts

These create a relatively simple visual representation of what may be a complex process. You might, for example, be reading about the development of a piece of equipment from its original conception (and the conditions in which it was conceived) to its production. A flow chart would allow you to break the whole process down into, for example, preliminary discussions, research phase, various forms of testing, final trials, production, operational application. Arrows leading from one phase to the next would trace a clear path through the process. It's a format that's useful in specific circumstances but it does need a lot of space and it may also have circuitous little flows weaving around the main one.

## Concept maps/mind-maps

In a way, these are a sort of 'flash-bang-wallop' style of note-making. The paper is usually set in landscape rather than the usual portrait format and ideas, concepts, statements are spread all over it with lines connecting those which might be linked together in terms of meaning or impact. The advantage is that they hold all the information on a single page, but they can get very messy as the information multiplies and there are sometimes so many points and lines that they're hard to follow. Before you use them in earnest, make sure that they're right for your particular learning style.

### Matrix notes/grid notes

Creating a table or matrix is obviously useful if your notes are recording different viewpoints, approaches, applications. It would, for example, be perfect if you were dealing with a problem that consisted of different elements and involved several contrasting viewpoints on those elements. An article on traffic problems might have separate columns for the views of the government, the police, local businesses, the local community. The various rows in the grid could then be labelled to test their attitudes to pedestrianisation, parking fees and fines, congestion charges, commercial access, car-sharing schemes. It gives a quick, easy-to-use overview of the issues and how they combine or contrast but there's not much space to develop notes or add extra information.

### Herringbone maps

This may sound a strange label but it's the perfect image for a format that lets you lay out opposing sides of an argument. Imagine the usual cartoon version of a fishbone, with a spine down the middle and bones sticking out on either side. On one side, the 'bones' carry statements for an argument, on the other are the statements against. It's simple and effective. But it's also limited. There's no obvious place for statements that are ambiguous or refer to things other than the for and against stances. And you might find you need a very long herring as you read more and more of the text and make more and more notes.

## Getting personal

We keep referring to books, articles and online sites as resources, but the same word applies to your notes. Never throw them away; you've spent lots of time collecting them and they may prove to be necessary, even important, if you change tack as your argument develops.

**brilliant** tip

Don't try to cram too much information onto a sheet. Leave white space around lists or other important items of information. It'll not only help you to remember the information more easily but also leave space for any extra details you might want to add later.

The visual aspects of your notes are important. They should be memorable, recognisable, designed in a way that shows you immediately the theme you're looking for. Be careful, though – don't turn the business of making them look good into a displacement activity. The idea isn't to make them look pretty or create some sort of art-form out of them, it's to create patterns, colours and shapes that trigger your recall and help you to organise them efficiently.

Find ways of abbreviating what you write. Use familiar abbreviations such as NATO or DNA and the common ones like e.g., i.e., etc., but develop your own shorthand too. You could use maths symbols, text-messaging techniques, or words from other languages. When we started writing this book, the word 'dissertation' was occurring quite frequently (naturally enough) so we used the Tools > AutoCorrect function to represent it with a single key – the hash sign. You can do the same thing with a pen – writing one little symbol instead of ten letters saves ages.

You can also save time by photocopying the relevant pages. This is useful if you don't need many notes on a particular topic or maybe when there's a lot of demand for a particular book and it's on short loan in the library. It's easier to get a photocopy and highlight the key bits or add your notes in the margins. In this case, though, it's important to remember that copyright law means that there are restrictions on photocopying. Check what they are by looking at notices in your library.

# What next?

### Look for a general dictionary ...

... that gives a comprehensive list of abbreviations and see which ones might be useful for you. Also, check a subject-specific dictionary for lists of specialist abbreviations. You'll not only be able to use them yourself but you'll know where to look if you come across one that's unfamiliar as you're reading.

### Everyone has a different method ...

... of note-making and we've actually suggested that you should personalise yours to suit your style. So compare your notes with those of a friend, on the same piece of text if possible. Talk about what you've chosen to note and why; it'll help both of you to appreciate any differences in reasoning, understanding or logic.

### Don't hesitate to try ...

... different styles. A strategy that works well for some things may be less good for others. Also, as you progress, the sorts of books you read may change and call for different approaches. So find a style that suits you but always be open to new things. Stay flexible.

**brilliant** recap

- Ask yourself why you're taking the notes and what should be in them.

- Understand the different ways of taking notes and try different formats for different exercises.

- Personalise your note-making with formatting tricks and abbreviations to make them easier to consult.

**PART 4**

Research
techniques

**CHAPTER 11**

# Quantitative research

Broadly speaking, there are two general categories of research – quantitative and qualitative. There are many variables within each of them and neither can be described as simple but, in general terms, quantitative research produces results in the form of numbers and is more commonly used in scientific project work. Both can be used for all disciplines and some investigations combine the two methods but in this chapter we'll concentrate on the quantitative method, its techniques and interpretations.

## The basics

The quantitative approach is useful for:

- getting measurements (for example, in biochemistry and physiology);
- estimating error (for example, in physics and engineering);
- comparing information and opinions (for example, sociology and psychology);
- and testing hypotheses (for example, in most investigative science disciplines).

Try to stay detached and make sure the results of the study are objective.

## The main features

Quantitative research is generally conclusive. It's especially important in the sciences, where its

___

quantitative research is generally conclusive

___

aim is often to provide a reliable value for a measurement or test a particular hypothesis. It can include:

- surveys and questionnaires ('Over 45 per cent of respondents agreed with this statement');

- measurements ('The average insect wing length was 3.40 mm with a standard error of 0.14 mm');

- experiments ('Treatment A resulted in a statistically significant increase in weight gain compared with the control').

The larger the sample you use, the more your measurements are likely to be representative of the population as a whole. You'll also have a better chance of reaching a conclusion that's statistically significant.

### brilliant definition

Population and sample are terms whose meanings are different from their 'normal' meanings (particularly in quantitative research).

**Population** – a defined group of items that might be part of a study: for example, all men in the UK; all individuals of a species of bivalve mollusc on a particular beach; all Birmingham householders who use gas as a heating fuel.

**Sample** – a sub-set of individuals from a specific population: for example, the 28 men whose blood sugar level was measured and compared with that of 34 who had taken drug X; the 50 bivalves collected from Beach A, measured and compared with a similar sample from Beach B; the 45 householders selected for telephone interview about their satisfaction with the service provided by their energy supplier.

## Methods

It's obvious that if you quantify your results they'll be less subjective. Observed numbers are, after all, 'facts' and not 'opinions' and therefore more likely to be objective. So you must make sure that your approach to data collection is unbiased. Bias can be defined as a partial or one-sided view or description of events and it can be introduced by faulty techniques. It may be that, for some subconscious reason, you select for observation or experiment individuals who don't truly represent the population. Alternatively, your values or measurements may be distorted, deliberately or accidentally.

### brilliant tip

Be careful when using the word or concept of 'proof' in quantitative research. It suggests you're 100 per cent certain and that's a level of certainty you can't really justify because statistical analysis and experimental design are inherently ambiguous. In reports and dissertations, use expressions such as 'this indicates that' rather than 'this proves that'.

### Surveys and questionnaires

These are valuable for getting quantitative as well as qualitative information. Respondents can be a representative sample (for example, members of the public chosen at random or using a sampling protocol) or a population (all members of Politics Class P201). The questions asked can be closed or open. The former are more useful for delivering data which can be interpreted numerically. The main types are:

- Categorical, which make respondents choose one option, for example: 'Gender: M/F'; or 'Do you agree with the above statement? – Yes/No/Don't know (delete as appropriate)'. In this case, the best way of expressing results is by using percentages.

- Numerical, which ask for a number as an answer, for example: 'What is your age in years?' You can summarise them using statistics of location and dispersion.

- Multiple-choice questions (MCQs), which are useful when there are mutually exclusive options and respondents have to 'tick one box'. It's easy to summarise them as percentages of respondents choosing each option.

- Multiple-response questions, which are like MCQs, except that respondents can choose more than one answer, for example: 'Which of the following resources have you used in the past month? (Tick all that apply)

  Hard-copy reference books

  Electronic encyclopaedia

  Textbooks

  Lecture handouts

  E-journals'

  These can also be summarised using percentages.

- Ranking (ordinal) questions, which ask respondents to place possible answers in an order, for example: 'Place the items in the following list in order of preference, writing 1 for your most preferred option, 2 for the next and so on, down to 5 for your least preferred option'.

- Likert-scale questions, which are useful for assessing people's opinions or feelings on a five-point scale. Typically, respondents are asked to react to a statement. An example would be: 'Which of the following best describes your feelings about the claim that smoking is dangerous for your health? (Circle the appropriate number.)

1 Agree strongly

2 Agree

3 Neither agree nor disagree

4 Disagree

5 Disagree strongly'

*Measurements and error*

A measurement is easy to define. In simple terms it's an estimate of some dimension of an object, such as 0.5 metres (abbreviated to m), 1.6 litres (l), 39 kilograms (kg). All measurements contain error, which can be of two types: accuracy, which indicates how close a measure or estimate is to its true value; or precision, which indicates how close repeated measurements are to each other. Most measurements are usually assumed to be accurate so the important thing is to find out how precise they are. There are two main ways of doing this:

● By establishing a range within which the measurement falls. If you're using a standard ruler, for example, you might give the result as 104 plus or minus 0.5 mm.

● By giving an estimated error based on repeated measurements of the same quantity. For example, if you weighed someone five times on the same machine, you could give the average of those five readings.

*Correlation*

This is a way of describing the relationship between two measured variables, such as the number of cigarettes smoked per day and life expectancy. A variable is well correlated with another if their values alter together, either in a positive fashion, or in a negative fashion, e.g. if life expectancy falls as tobacco consumption rises.

However, it's very important not to assume that correlation implies a direct link between cause and effect. If A is well correlated with B, that doesn't in itself mean that A causes B. The real cause could be something connected with A, or even, due to coincidence, something completely different. If people with high blood pressure are more likely to have heart attacks, this alone doesn't 'prove' that high blood pressure is a cause of heart attacks. The only way to become more certain is to gather more evidence.

### Experiments

An experiment is a situation which you create to try to isolate the effects of changing one variable in a system or process. You can then compare the results with the condition where there's been no change. The aim behind many experiments is to show that a change in factor A causes a change in variable B, or maybe to examine in more detail how A causes B. Experiments are at the core of the 'scientific method' which is designed to allow a hypothesis to be accepted or rejected.

## Results

These various methods, and the data, statistics or results they generate, aren't enough in themselves; you have to show that you understand them and can apply critical thinking to interpret them and arrive at conclusions or hypotheses. When you come to do that, there are several things to bear in mind.

### Statistics plus

Quantitative research usually gathers information from large unbiased samples to make sure that the sample is representative of the population as a whole, and to increase the chances of reaching a statistically significant conclusion. But statistics on their own aren't enough. The results of observations, surveys or experiments need to be analysed and it's your analytical and presentational skills that may lift your marks when your dissertation or report is being assessed.

### The limits of statistics

Statistical techniques let you compare sets of observations or treatments to test hypotheses and to indicate the probability of your conclusions being right or wrong. They're powerful tools but just because you can measure something, or compare data sets, that's no guarantee that your conclusions will be certain or relevant. Don't forget that many scientists accept that there's a 5 per cent chance of their conclusions being wrong. Then again, even if a hypothesis is accepted as correct, the results may apply only to that specific, highly artificial experimental or observational environment. So don't confuse statistical significance with 'importance' or 'value'.

> because you can measure something that's no guarantee that your conclusions will be certain or relevant

### The importance of 'Materials and methods'

You must describe your methods fully because one goal of quantitative research is to produce repeatable results from which general conclusions can be drawn. Your 'Materials and methods' section should contain enough information to allow a competent peer to repeat your work.

### Make it clear

Pay as much attention to the language you use to describe your experiments and convey your results and conclusions as you do to the figures and measurements. Keep it clear and unambiguous, and define any qualitative terms you use as precisely as possible. You might, for example, convey the colour of a specimen by referring to a standard colour chart.

The same advice applies to designing surveys. Don't assume that the respondents will react in the same way as you do. For example, if you write: 'Do you agree with this statement? Yes/no', is the respondent supposed to circle the answer they agree with, cross out the one they disagree with, or make some other sort of mark? If in doubt, check how others have worded their questions and instructions.

## Some practical advice

*Surveys*

- Try out the questions on a friend or family member before starting with real subjects.

- Keep the survey as short as possible.

- Get the appropriate demographic information to describe your sample and make correlations.

- Start with general questions and move on to specific ones.

- When explaining how your survey was conducted, supply appropriate details, including:

  - sampling methods – how you contacted or chose the respondents and what ethical procedures you followed;

  - details of respondents;

  - how you designed and administered the questionnaire.

### brilliant tip

Unless your study is about language and its inaccuracies, correct your respondents' grammar and spelling errors and add a note to the 'Materials and methods' section to explain that you've done so.

*Experiments*

Think about the method of statistical analysis you'll be using first of all. It may influence how you design the experiment. Keep your experiments simple, make some trial runs of them to see that they do what you intended, and always keep safety issues in mind.

## What next?

**Plan a survey or experiment ...**

... or the procedures necessary for a measurement so that the different steps in the process are clear to you. Don't forget to consider things that might restrict your resources, such as how much time you can expect respondents to give you; or, for an experiment, whether test subjects or equipment will be available. Think about and make a list of any potential forms of bias in your research; it'll help you avoid them.

### Find out what statistical tests ...

... you can do using the software available to you. Will a spreadsheet program like Excel be enough, or will you need a more sophisticated program? The more initial preparation you do, the easier the actual work will be.

## brilliant recap

- Use quantitative methods and techniques for research whose results are generally produced as numbers.

- Make sure your surveys, questionnaires and experiments are precise in their focus. Phrase questions and interpret results with care.

- Use critical thinking to arrive at your conclusions; interpret statistics with care and recognise their limits.

- Make sure the language you use to describe results is unambiguous.

- Follow this practical advice when designing surveys.

**CHAPTER 12**

# Qualitative
# research

Qualitative research uses investigative approaches that produce results in the form of descriptive textual information. It tends to be used more in the arts disciplines but it's important to remember that the two methods aren't mutually exclusive. Both can be used for all disciplines and some investigations even combine the two. In this chapter we'll look at the broad basics of qualitative research and its techniques for interpreting information.

## The basics

In general terms, the qualitative approach is for investigating:

- opinions, feelings, and values (for example, in political science, social policy, philosophy);
- people's interpretations and responses (for example, in sociology, psychology);
- behavioural patterns (for example, in ethnography, anthropology, geography);
- processes and patterns (for example, in education, economics, accountancy);
- case studies including critical incidents (for example, in nursing, education).

You then interpret your results according to your own values and intentions. The approach is generally exploratory. It's especially important in the social sciences, where the aim is often to understand the complexities of human behaviour. This type of research can include:

● case studies ('Student X described her experience on her first day at university as …');

● interviews ('Interviewee A explained that, after seeing the video, his reaction was … This could be interpreted as …');

● focus groups ('One group member stated that her experience of peer marking was …').

## Methods

By its very nature, qualitative research implies a degree of bias, so it's just as important to remain objective in the way you conduct it as it is when you're reporting your findings.

**by its very nature, qualitative research implies a degree of bias**

It generally involves individuals or small, carefully selected samples. These may not be representative of the population as a whole, but that's not necessarily important because the value of this sort of investigation lies in its authentic, case-specific detail. The information you get is potentially richer and deeper than the sort you get from numbers and statistics, and opinions, experiences and feelings can be expressed in many subtle ways. The downside of this is that, while they're complex, subtle and individual, it's less easy to make comparisons between different cases and arrive at generalised conclusions.

**brilliant** definition

These appeared in the previous chapter but they're relevant to both types of research and so it's worth repeating them.

Population and sample are terms whose meanings are different from their 'normal' meanings (particularly in quantitative research).

**Population** – a defined group of items that might be part of a study: for example, all men in the UK; all individuals of a species of bivalve mollusc on a particular beach; all Birmingham householders who use gas as a heating fuel.

**Sample** – a sub-set of individuals from a specific population: for example, the 28 men whose blood sugar level was measured and compared with that of 34 who had taken drug X; the 50 bivalves collected from Beach A, measured and compared with a similar sample from Beach B; the 45 householders selected for telephone interview about their satisfaction with the service provided by their energy supplier.

## *Observation and description*

This is when you examine an artefact, person or location and describe it. You might also trace developments through time. It's the method you'd use for investigating such topics as:

- primary source material such as that found in an historical document;
- a biological habitat;
- a patient's symptoms;
- a drawing, painting or installation.

Description is sometimes seen as a 'lower-level' academic thought process, but the interpretations and generalisations that are needed to interpret it further depend on distinctly higher-level skills.

## Surveys and questionnaires

We outlined the various types of surveys and questionnaires you could use in the previous chapter and those remarks apply for both quantitative and qualitative research. The main qualitative technique is to ask an 'open' question, for example 'What do you think about the new property valuation system?' or 'Do you have any further comments?' They can produce answers from a quite complex mini-speech to total silence but they do provide authentic quotes which illustrate representative and/or opposing points of view and can thus give your work more interest and colour.

When organising your interview questions, make sure you don't lead the respondent by asking some question early on which might put a particular idea or concept in his mind and affect his response to a later question. Try to start with general questions or prompts and move to the specific.

Once again, for those of you who may have skipped the previous chapter because you were less interested in a quantitative approach, there are some basic techniques we need to repeat. If you're conducting a survey, make sure your instructions are clear. If you write: 'Do you agree with this statement? Yes/No', some people may circle the answer they agree with, others may score out the one they disagree with (and the scoring out might resemble a tick of approval), and some may make marks which baffle you completely. To iron out problems of that nature, try getting a friend or family member to take the survey before using it on real subjects.

**make sure your instructions are clear**

The basic survey rules are:

- Keep it as short as possible. Use the minimum number of questions you need to get the relevant information and only ask a question if you know exactly how you'll use the answer.

- Collect the appropriate demographic information to describe your sample and draw correlations.

- Make sure your questions are unambiguous.

- In deciding the order of questions, try to move from the general to the specific so that there's less chance of early questions influencing responses to later ones.

### brilliant definition

**Correlation** – the strength and direction of the relationship between two variables.

**Variable** – a mathematical quantity that can take different values in different cases.

Part of your dissertation or report will consist of a description of how the survey was conducted. This should include:

- Sampling methods. How did you contact and choose the respondents? What ethical procedures did you follow?

- Details of respondents. You should provide a summary of demographics (the gender, age and background of those responding). You can get these details from questions, usually at the start of the survey, but it's important to reassure respondents that their privacy and anonymity will be protected.

- Questionnaire design. Discuss the principles and rationale behind it and include a copy in your submission as an appendix.

- Procedure. How did you carry out the survey?

It's normal to correct your respondents' grammar and spelling errors because the important thing is to convey the spirit of what they wrote rather than divert the reader's attention by careless mistakes. Add a note to the 'Material and methods' section to explain that you've done this.

*Interview-based case studies*

Qualitative research often draws on individuals' experiences of events, processes and systems. These can be reported as case studies. In theory, the best way of carrying out this type of investigation without your own preconceptions getting in the way would be to allow the participant to provide a completely unstructured and uninterrupted stream of thought. You'd then draw your conclusions after examining and reflecting on it all. In practice, though, it makes more sense (and it certainly makes your task easier) if you use prior knowledge and experience (your own and that acquired from your reading) to structure an interview by creating a series of prompting questions. If you use a similar structure for each case study, you'll be able to compare results more easily.

*Action Research*

You're sometimes encouraged to undertake studies focusing on local issues, particularly in the 'caring' disciplines such as nursing, social work and teaching. In such instances a popular approach is Action Research, which involves studying a problem or situation which requires better understanding and, possibly, identifying some change to resolve the problem or improve the situation.

*Focus groups*

These are small discussion groups (ideally of 4–6 members), where participants are asked to comment on an issue or, if it's in a commercial context, a product or marketing tool. You can gather several viewpoints at a time and observe the outcomes of open and dynamic discussion among the group members. You need to be careful not to introduce bias by leading the discussion yourself, and also to watch out for any tendency amongst group members to stick to the middle ground because they're shy about expressing a minority opinion.

**brilliant** tip

Make sure you have a list of discussion topics or questions prepared which relate to your research interest. Be ready to intervene in discussions to introduce a new topic or bring participants back to the point if they start drifting into irrelevant side issues.

## Practical tips

● Achieve a balance.
   When you've collected the information you need, the important thing is to organise and present it in a balanced, rational way. Don't be tempted to choose only examples, answers or quotes that support your view. Include the

opposing evidence as well, then conduct a careful analysis of the arguments and literature sources you've consulted to arrive at a conclusion.

● Be comprehensive.
As soon as you can, gather all your sources together and scan-read them to get a quick overview before you start describing and comparing them. Always note down more information than you think you'll need. You can get rid of irrelevant material later but you can't always go back to find information you missed first time round.

● Choose with care.
Choose your interviewees or members of focus groups carefully. Discuss with your supervisor what the criteria should be, then screen participants accordingly. You might, for example, want to interview people involved at all stages in a process (shop-floor, administrative, management, marketing and customer); or a balanced set of students of both sexes and representing different levels of study. You'll need to give the details of the selection criteria in your report.

● Make the most of meetings.
For group discussions, think about the best seating arrangement. Make sure everyone is comfortable, introduce yourself and say what the meeting is for. It helps if you use nametags or labels of some sort to make things less impersonal. As well as noting what the people in the group say, be aware of other signals, such as facial expressions, eye contact, tone of voice and body language. If you add notes about these, it may help with your interpretations.

## What next?

### Whether you're writing ...

... a description, conducting a focus group or carrying out a case study, try to find a published study which used a similar technique. Analyse its approach and methods to see whether you can use or adapt them for your own investigation. Study the ways its results have been presented to see if they'd be suitable for you to use.

**If you intend using ...**

... interviews and focus groups, plan a set of question 'prompts' and possible 'question probes' which will encourage respondents to discuss the points they're making in greater depth.

## brilliant recap

- Qualitative research is used to investigate such things as opinions, behaviours and case studies. Its results are usually expressed as descriptive textual information.

- Be aware of the different methods of acquiring information and the importance of remaining objective in interpreting it.

- Design surveys, questionnaires and interviews with care and frame questions so that they're clear for respondents and provide relevant answers.

- Learn the basic uses of case studies, action research and focus groups.

- Use sound techniques when conducting the research and interpreting the results.

**CHAPTER 13**

# Experiments and field trips

Your research, especially in the sciences and non-scientific subjects such as geography and psychology, will probably include laboratory sessions and/or field visits. They're just as important as the things you find in your research literature and they're perfect for observing specimens, getting more familiar with standard procedures and refining your various research skills. They're also specialised environments, so you need to do things safely, follow the rules and make sure your data collection is accurate.

## Hands-on research

The practical aspects of your research call for a different set of skills and help you to widen your approach to the topic. You get to interact with real examples of organisms, specimens, artefacts, processes and reactions and refine your techniques of observation, measurement, manipulation and data analysis. Designing, carrying out and reporting original experiments gives you a better appreciation of 'scientific method' and lets you learn how best to use the various items of equipment. You also get practice in writing up your work in formats that'll be very useful when it's time to report your project or write theses at a higher level. More generally, you'll learn the importance of working safely, the techniques of data analysis, how to create tables and graphs and the demands and benefits of working as part of a team.

## Preparation

To get the most from practical research, you need to prepare for it properly. Your lab sessions and field trips will probably be tightly scheduled and you may have to get going right from the start. There may be new concepts and terms to learn so, before you begin, find out all you can about them.

> to get the most from practical research, you need to prepare for it properly

- Read carefully any instructions or papers you've been given.
- Make sure you've got the right equipment ready for the job.
- Check the research process to see if you need any specialist equipment and, if you do, reserve it so that it's available when you need it.

## How to behave in the lab and field

Safety's always the first consideration so it's crucial to follow all the rules laid down about your lab or fieldwork. Where people are working with toxic chemicals, dangerous instruments or in hazardous environments, everyone must be very careful. If you're not certain about basic safety measures, fire drills, emergency procedures and what you must and mustn't do, find out right away. Also, learn or remind yourself of the basic warning symbols for things such as fire, harmful, irritant or toxic substances, flammable or corrosive materials and any others you're likely to come across in your work. You'll find examples in Figure 13.1.

### *Personal protection*

In the lab, wear a lab coat, keep it buttoned up and, if your hair's long, tie it back. You may sometimes need eye protection goggles and, if you wear contact lenses, be on the lookout for special rules because vapours from corrosive chemicals can get trapped between the lens and your eye.

Explosive

Oxidising agent

Extremely or
highly flammable

Toxic or very toxic

Corrosive

Harmful or irritant

Dangerous for
the environment

**Figure 13.1** Some of the main EU hazard symbols

*Source*: McMillan & Weyers: *How to Write Dissertations and Project Reports*, Prentice Hall, 2010.

### Working habits

So safety's a priority; most of its features are simply common sense and should be second nature to you anyway, but never make assumptions. Don't take any procedures, equipment or the environment itself for granted. Familiarity can breed carelessness so develop good, safe working habits:

● Never eat or smoke in a lab.

● Keep your bench space tidy.

● Dispose of specimens or sharps quickly and in the right way.

● If the work involves a COSHH risk assessment, you'll be told about it and you must read it carefully.

**brilliant** definition

**COSHH** – This stands for 'Control of Substances Hazardous to Health'. It's a UK regulation that came into force in 1999. It lays out the legal framework for risk assessment whenever hazardous chemicals, agents or procedures are used. Normally the person in charge of your lab or field visit (your supervisor or a senior lab technician) carries out a COSHH assessment. You'll be briefed on it and it may be displayed prominently so that it's easy for everyone to consult it.

### Emergencies and responses

Working with chemicals or live organisms such as bacteria calls for special precautions. There are several ways they could get inside you – breathing them in, swallowing them, or simply absorbing them through exposed skin, cuts or scratches. So when you're using pipettes or transferring samples between vessels, take special care. Before you start, find out where the eye washes and emergency showers are in your lab, and make sure you know what to do if you do come into contact with or spill any chemicals. In each location, note where the fire extinguishers or fire blankets are and what types you should use for the reagents you're working with. And, when you've finished in the lab, wash your hands thoroughly.

### Field visits

You should get some advice about what to wear for field visits. The right footwear's important and, whatever the weather's like when you set out, remember that it can change quite quickly. Check the forecast and if you're going to be working on the seashore find out about the state of the tides. Always try to work with a partner, take a first aid kit, and leave details of where you're going and when you'll be back.

### Instructions and results

When the procedures for lab work and field visits are listed, they usually deal first with theory, background and aims, then with detailed instructions. Don't be tempted to jump straight to the instructions because you must first be sure about the nature of the work and what it's trying to achieve. When you do move on to the instructions, you'll probably find that they spell things out very specifically for you and it's your job to do exactly as they say. Measuring reagents precisely or getting your timings and temperatures exactly right, for example, will make all the difference to the accuracy of your results. As part of your preparation, you could highlight key points in the instructions to make it easier to follow them during the session, or you could lay out tables ready for your data.

## brilliant tip

There are certain conventions to follow when you're writing practical reports. In the 'Introduction' and 'Materials and methods' sections, you should generally use the past tense, passive voice and third person (for example, 'Sturrock and Dodds (1984) were the first to show ...' and 'the data were recorded at 5-minute intervals'). You can, though, use the present tense to refer to figures and tables (for example, 'Table 3 shows the relationship between ...'). The best way to get a feel for the style to use is to read some research reports in your own subject area.

### Observing and recording

It's obvious that you need to record what you see and measure as accurately as possible. As you're working, don't just think you'll remember things, write them down. Use a proper lab book, not scraps of paper – you're bound to lose them. Put the date on each page and give full details of the specimen or experiment.

record what you see and measure as accurately as possible

If it's data you're recording, write it down clearly. The numbers 1 and 7, for example, are easily confused so it might be an idea to use the continental style and cross the stem of the 7. Make sure your final answers or results are written in the form usually used in your discipline. If you're using diagrams, describe and label them with care and draw graphs and tables according to the normal scientific conventions. As a precaution against bad weather, buy a special wet-weather notebook or cover your usual one with a clear plastic bag. Use a pencil, too; it's better on damp paper than pens or biros.

It's worth reminding yourself of the breakdown of a typical lab report and what you expect to find in the various sections.

| Section or part | Expected content |
| --- | --- |
| Title page | The full names of the author or authors, the module title or code, the date, and a descriptive title that says what you've done and maybe describes the 'headline' finding. |
| Abstract | A brief summary of the aims of the experiment or series of observations; the main outcomes (in words) and conclusions. This is to help the reader to understand your main findings and what you think they mean. |
| Abbreviations | A list of abbreviations for technical terms you've used (for example, 'DNA: deoxyribonucleic acid'). You should also write these in brackets after the word or expression occurs for the first time in your text, for example '... deoxyribonucleic acid (DNA)'. |
| Introduction | An outline of the background to the project, the aims of the experiment(s) or observations and brief discussion of the techniques you'll be using. This lets the reader know what to expect and says what you've done and why you've done it. |
| Materials and methods | A description of what was done. There should be enough detail for a competent person to be able to repeat the work. |
| Results | A description of the data obtained, usually presented in tables or graphs (but never both for the same data). You needn't present the data in the same order in which you did the work but it might be helpful to highlight any aspects which you think are particularly significant. |
| Discussion | A commentary on the results and an outline of the main conclusions. This could include any or all of the following: <br><br>• Comments on the methods used <br>• Mention of sources of errors <br>• Conclusions from any statistical analysis <br>• Comparison with other findings or the 'ideal' result <br>• What the result means <br>• How you might improve the methods used <br>• Where you would go from here if you had more time and resources. <br><br>Sometimes you might want to combine this section with the previous one on results. You could then develop a narrative which, for example, could explain why one result led to the next experiment or approach. Remember that your original thoughts in this section could earn you a large proportion of the overall marks. |
| Acknowledgements | A list of people who helped you. |
| References | An alphabetical list of sources cited in the text, following one of the standard formats. |

## brilliant dos and don'ts

### Do

✔ use lab assistants and senior researchers. They may be recent graduates so they'll understand and be sympathetic to any problems you're having. If in doubt, don't wait to be asked, be prepared to ask questions yourself.

✔ learn how to draw up informal tables and figures quickly. Rough tables will help you to record your results, and 'instant' graphs will give you a quick visual indication of how the experiment's going.

✔ include a column in your tables to describe what's being measured or the number or timing of the measurements, and make sure there are enough cells in the rows for each measurement.

✔ assess the largest and smallest figures you're likely to get when you're making a graph so that you can decide what the limits of the graph axes should be.

✔ state the measured quantity and the units of measurement for all tables and figures, no matter how quickly you've sketched them.

✔ take lots of notes and provide detailed labels, adding time and date. As well as just saying what something is, add details such as colour and texture and remember to include a scale with all diagrams.

✔ use most of your senses, but with caution: note colours, sounds and feel, but only taste and smell when you're specifically instructed to.

✔ use 'dead' time effectively – that means any delays between parts of your work as reactions develop, or as instruments complete a process. While you wait, use the time to think about what you'll be doing next, create tables or graphs ready for your results, or jot down ideas for your conclusions.

✔ write up your practical work while it's still fresh in your mind. You may be tired after a lengthy lab session, but if you leave it until later, you may forget useful details.

# What next?

### Make a checklist ...

... of items you'll need for each experiment or field visit.

### Rehearse safety scenarios ...

... using the safety information in the relevant lab handbooks, lab notices and your supervisor's advice. Imagine what you'd do in different emergency situations such as a fire, someone swallowing a toxic chemical, someone cutting himself. It'll increase your awareness of the dangers of lab and fieldwork and help you react faster if ever you need to.

### Buy and organise ...

... a lab notebook. It's vital for both lab and fieldwork researchers. A hardback notebook is best. Date each entry and use the book to record details of your experiments, observations, results and ideas. When you can, write up each part more formally using a word processor or spreadsheet.

## brilliant recap

- Prepare properly for all practical work. Practise detailed safety awareness, cultivate good safe working habits and use the correct personal protection.

- Know what to do in an emergency in the lab and/or on field trips.

- Be professional in your observations and recording of results. Use this example of a typical lab report for guidance.

- The checklist of suggestions will make your tasks easier, your overall working methods more efficient and your results reliable.

**CHAPTER 14**

# The importance of critical thinking

The ability to think critically is probably the most valuable skill you'll develop at university. It's an ability with uses and applications in all walks of work and life and it's particularly important when you're writing up a research project. So we need to do some thinking about thinking.

## A logical approach to analysis and problem-solving

Is it actually possible to think better? Are there theories or techniques that can help? Well, most university teaching is based on the assumption that you can and there are. Basically, you need to recognise what it is and practise it.

You won't get good results simply by having a good memory, recalling facts and churning them out. You need to analyse and synthesise facts, reach an opinion about them and support it with evidence and argument. If you're systematic and methodical about doing this, it'll help with all sorts of tasks, from the easy to the more challenging.

> if you're systematic and methodical it'll help with all sorts of tasks

## brilliant definition

**Critical thinking**: The first reaction to the words 'critical' and 'criticism' is usually to assume they're negative. But critical thinking is positive. It means considering all aspects of a topic and then making a careful judgement about it. Critical thinking is good, creative thinking.

## Thinking about thinking

A famous educational psychologist, Benjamin Bloom, and some of his colleagues listed six steps in learning and thinking in education:

- knowledge
- comprehension
- application
- analysis
- synthesis
- evaluation.

Their analysis was very detailed but for our purposes it's enough to understand what these different phases mean in more general terms. They can be seen as a natural progression. It's probably obvious, for example, that the things you did at school involved mainly knowledge, comprehension and application. At university, you've needed to do more analysis, synthesis and evaluation and that higher-order thinking is even more critical now that you're faced with your own extended piece of research.

Basically, you need knowledge, understanding and an ability to apply both in different contexts. You have to look more deeply into ideas and theories, bring different thoughts together and make judgements about the results. In other words, you must be able to analyse, synthesise and evaluate different viewpoints or approaches, and look at issues from different perspectives. As you do so, you can set your own criteria and use them to examine strong and weak lines of argument in what you read and use evidence from the literature to support your own findings.

## brilliant example

### Knowledge

If you know a fact, you can recall or recognise it but you don't necessarily understand it at a higher level. So the words 'Define', 'Describe', 'Identify' and similar expressions are asking you to use knowledge.

### Comprehension

Comprehending a fact means that you do understand what it means, which puts you in a position to 'Contrast', 'Discuss' or 'Interpret'.

### Application

Knowing and understanding a fact means you know how to use or 'apply' it to 'Demonstrate', 'Calculate' or 'Illustrate'.

### Analysis

The next step is being able to break knowledge down into parts and show how they fit together, so you can 'Analyse', 'Explain' and 'Compare'.

### Synthesis

Synthesising is the ability to select relevant facts from your knowledge and use them in different ways or different contexts to create something new. That's what you need to do when asked to 'Compose', 'Create' or 'Integrate'.

### Evaluation

After all of that, you're in a position to evaluate facts and information and arrive at a judgement. You can then 'Recommend', 'Support' and 'Draw a conclusion'.

---

Be careful, though. This isn't a set of fixed 'rules'. For example, if you're asked to 'Describe' something in the sciences, you may simply have to note what you observe – element A was added to element B and resulted in reaction X. The same word in architecture, however, might call for much more complex skills and theoretical perspectives.

## The 'six steps' in practice

In order to illustrate more clearly the nature of the different phases, let's apply them to three general types of discipline – law, arts subjects, numerical subjects. These are just examples and you need to decide which stages are relevant and/or useful for you and the type of research you're doing. You can accept or reject phases, change their order – in other words, you should adapt them to create a model which meets your specific needs.

### Law

**Knowledge** – you know the name and date of a case, statute or treaty but don't understand its relevance.

**Comprehension** – you understand both the principle of law in the legislation or case and its wider context.

**Application** – you're able to identify situations to which the principle would apply.

**Analysis** – you can see how the facts of a particular scenario relate to the principle and use that knowledge to uncover the extent of its application.

**Synthesis** – using reasoning and analogy, you can predict how the law might be applied in other circumstances.

**Evaluation** – you're able to consider the various options and use your judgement as a basis for advising a client.

### Arts, e.g. history or politics

**Knowledge** – you know that a river is an important geographical and political boundary in international relations, but you don't know why.

**Comprehension** – you understand that the river forms a natural barrier, which can be easily identified and defended.

**Application** – you can use this knowledge to explain the terms of a peace treaty.

**Analysis** – you can see that the fact that the river is a boundary is important for signatories to the peace treaty in terms of their possible gains or losses of territory.

**Synthesis** – you can relate this awareness to the recurrence of the same issue in later treaties and its possible implications.

**Evaluation** – you can discuss whether this boundary was an obstacle to resolving the terms of the treaty to the satisfaction of all parties.

*Numerical subjects*

**Knowledge** – you can write down a particular mathematical equation, without understanding what the symbols mean or where it might be applied.

**Comprehension** – you understand what the symbols mean and how and when to apply the equation.

**Application** – if you have the background information you can use the equation to obtain a result.

**Analysis** – you can explain the theoretical process involved in deriving the equation.

**Synthesis** – you can take one equation, link it with another and arrive at a new mathematical relationship or conclusion.

**Evaluation** – you can discuss the limitations of an equation based on its derivation and the underlying assumptions behind this.

## A system for critical thinking

OK, so you have a particular problem and you feel that critical thinking will help you solve it. It could be anything from working out a conclusion for your research to deciding what type of car to buy or where to rent a flat. Every type of problem becomes more manageable if you approach it logically and organise your thinking in a methodical way. The approach suggested below isn't itself a solution; it simply identifies stages you might go through to reach a conclusion. Reject them, adapt them, change their order but think about them and get what suits you best from them.

### What's the problem?

First of all, you need to be sure that there really is a problem or that it really is what you think it is rather than something else. Write down a description of it and be very precise with your wording. If it's a question of interpreting a specific title, analyse its phrasing carefully, look for alternative meanings.

### How do you approach it?

Try some 'brainstorming' to identify possible solutions or viewpoints. Start with some general, 'open' thinking, move to the organisation phase, then progress to analysis.

Look at it from all possible angles and write down everything you come up with, even if you're not sure it's relevant or important. If you use a 'spider diagram' or 'mind-map', that might help you to make associations and multiply the ideas you're having.

When you're satisfied that you've had a thorough go at exploring lots of ideas, try to arrange them into categories or sub-headings. Alternatively, you could group them as arguments for and against a particular viewpoint. A new diagram, table or grid might be useful at this stage.

Once you've got them relatively organised, you can start eliminating the ones that are trivial or irrelevant and sort the rest into some sort of order of priority.

*Back up the information with evidence*

Now that you've narrowed (or maybe broadened) your focus, make sure you understand the facts. You'll probably need to collect more information and ideas to extend your response, so find some examples or suggest a range of interpretations or approaches which support your viewpoint. You might only need to use dictionaries and technical works to find out the precise meaning of key words; or you might discuss your ideas with your peers or your supervisor; or you could read a few texts to see what other people have said about the topic.

*Assemble your case*

You've gathered lots of information, so it's time to make sure it's all relevant and does apply to your question. Look at the question again, check that you really do understand it, and start organising what you've collected. Some of it will support your argument, some of it will oppose it. Maybe a table or grid would help you to get it organised and see the balance you have between for and against. If any of the material is dubious, get rid of it. You want the strongest possible case, with no trivial or irrelevant distractions.

*Build to a conclusion*

By this stage, you've done so much thinking about it and gathered so much material that you'll probably have formed a strong personal viewpoint. What you have to do now is build your dissertation or report around it. You know what you want to say, so just say it. But be careful. It's too easy to slip into making value judgements or using other terms or expressions of opinion that aren't supported by the evidence you have.

## Beware value judgements

Value judgements are statements that reflect the views and values of an individual rather than any objective reality. Someone who supports a cause calls it a pressure group; but to a person who disagrees with it, its followers are 'activists'. 'Conservationists' may be called 'tree-huggers'; 'freedom fighters' may be 'terrorists' and vice versa. The words don't just have a meaning, they imply an attitude and quite often, it's negative. In a discussion, how valuable or 'true' is the claim that 'Teenagers are unreliable, unpredictable and unable to accept responsibility for their actions'? Value judgements are subjective, often biased opinions. It's important for your conclusions to be objective and supported by facts.

## brilliant definition

**A fallacy** – a fault in logic or thinking that means that an argument is incorrect.

**Bias** – information that emphasises just one viewpoint or position.

**Propaganda** – false or incomplete information that supports a (usually) extreme political or moral view.

## Fallacies and biased presentations

Critical thinking demands a sensitivity to language. Arguments and discussions are mostly reasoned, dispassionate affairs but even in such contexts, the choice of words reveals more than the speaker or writer sometimes suspects. If you can spot them, you'll be able to think not just about the argument itself but also about the way it's being conducted. If troops are massing on a border, it's legitimate to talk of them being a 'threat'. But if you add the word 'sinister', you're making assumptions about the reasons why they're moving into position and speculating on their intentions. In other words, you're not just an observer but someone who's becoming involved in the processes taking place.

The obvious areas in which faulty logic and debating tricks are used are those of advertising and politics. Analysing the methods of persuasion and misdirection they use is a useful way of practising your critical skills.

As well as being aware of how others use words, try to balance your own style and choose your words with care. It's very easy to slip into bad habits. 'Absolutes' such as 'always', 'never', 'all', 'every' are such familiar expressions that we can use them without really thinking of how they affect our meaning. Each of them means that there are no exceptions. You should only use them if you're absolutely sure of facts that imply 100 per cent certainty.

## A review of critical thinking

- It should be obvious by now that critical thinking is a practical, hands-on process, not just abstract theorising. So make sure you appreciate and apply those practical aspects. Focus on the task in hand. Once you start reading around a subject or discussing it with others, it's easy to get distracted and stray from the point.

- Write down your thoughts. As you do so, you'll be forced to clarify them and maybe refine them. Apart from that, even though we think we'll remember a good idea, it often drifts away and we can't recall it. So make it permanent; write it down. As you review it later, you'll see it more critically and it can lead you to fresh ideas.

- Don't content yourself with just quoting facts or statements, without trying to explain their importance and context or even say why you've included them. That could suggest that you maybe don't understand what a quotation means or implies. Your work will be more interesting and persuasive if it's analytical, not descriptive.

- When you do quote evidence from other sources, it's very important to use appropriate citations. This shows you've read relevant source material and helps you to avoid plagiarism. Make sure you find out which style conventions your university uses and be consistent in how you use them.

- Refresh and expand your own ideas by discussing things with others – staff and students. They might have interpretations and opinions which haven't occurred to you. Bounce ideas off one another.

- Keep an open mind. You may start with preconceived ideas or sound convictions about a topic, but try still to be receptive to the ideas of others. You may find that your conviction isn't as secure as you first thought.

- And if there's not enough evidence to support any conclusion, say so. There may well be times when both sides of an argument are equally valid. Recognising that is as valid as deciding that one side or the other is 'correct'.

Critical thinking isn't just an academic exercise, it's about who you are. Shallow thinkers rush to conclusions, generalise, over-simplify. They make the arguments personal, resort to stereotypes, make value judgements and hide behind fallacies. Their results are usually inconclusive and unsatisfactory.

> critical thinking isn't just an academic exercise, it's about who you are

To think more deeply you need to keep asking yourself questions, even if the topic's been sorted out or you feel you understand it. Look beneath the surface. Decide whether the sources you're using are dealing with facts or opinions; look out for assumptions, including your own; think about why writers write the way they do. And when you quote from a source, don't just repeat what it's saying, focus on what it really means.

# What next?

**Practise seeing ...**

... both sides of an argument. Choose a topic, maybe something you feel strongly about. Write down the supporting arguments for both sides, paying particular attention to the arguments opposite to your own.

**Look into the often entertaining world ...**

... of fallacies and biased arguments. There are websites that list different types of them with examples. Just type 'fallacy' or 'logical fallacies' into a search engine; you'll learn from what you read, it'll help to improve your analytical and debating skills. And it'll probably make you laugh.

**brilliant** recap

- Critical thinking is good, creative thinking.

- There are six steps in learning and thinking: knowledge, comprehension, application, analysis, synthesis, evaluation.

- Understand the various steps – identify the problem, decide on an approach, build a case, use supporting evidence, draw your conclusion.

- Avoid pitfalls such as faulty logic and bias.

# PART 5

# Numbers and data

**CHAPTER 15**

# Working with numbers

I f your project involves quantitative research, you'll probably have to use some maths. It's a varied discipline with all sorts of aspects so if you're having to do things involving numbers and symbols with which you aren't familiar, it's best to read about the concepts and methods and practise using them. Your supervisor may be able to help you or tell you where to look for solutions to the problem, but she'll expect you to at least try to get the answers for yourself first of all.

> it's best to read about the concepts and methods and practise using them

## Arithmetic and algebra

It's not just maths itself which calls for an ability to handle numbers and symbols. Subjects such as biology, economics, geography, psychology and many others can also require numerical skills. This chapter isn't intended to provide a comprehensive crash course in maths but, if you haven't used it for a while, it'll try to remind you of the basics which you may need.

### Numbers and symbols

The language of maths consists of numbers and symbols, both of which have their own special 'vocabulary'. So first, you need to know what the various 'words' mean. Let's start with some basic terms.

## Constants and variables

Constants are values which never change, such as gravitational acceleration ($g$) or *pi* ($\pi$). You'll often find them in tables, but sometimes you just have to memorise them. Variables are mathematical quantities that can take different values. In other words, as their name suggests, they can change.

In the familiar formula for the circumference of a circle, $2\pi r$, *pi* never changes but $r$ (the radius of the circle) does according to the size of the circle. And if someone's bouncing on a trampoline, the height of their jumps may change but the gravitational force that brings them back down remains constant.

### brilliant definition

Numbers are classified in sets:

Whole numbers: 0, 1, 2, 3 ...

Natural numbers: 1, 2, 3, 4 ...

Integers: $-2$, $-1$, 0, 1, 2, 3 ...

Real numbers: integers and anything in between, e.g. 1.54, $\pi$, $e^4$.

Prime numbers: natural numbers that can only be divided by themselves and 1.

Rational numbers: $p/q$, where $p$ is an integer and $q$ is natural and there's no common factor.

Irrational numbers: real numbers with no exact value, such as $\pi$. If the final digit is repeated, it's often written as $4/3 = 1.3$ or 1.3r.

## Units

Constants and variables can be just numbers, abstract things without any dimensions. But most of them do have units, such as metres (m), metres per second squared (m s$^{-2}$), or kilograms (kg). There's a list of agreed standard units which are used in all the sciences. It's called the *Système International d'Unités*, or SI.

## Prefixes

We often use prefixes to indicate very large and very small numbers. 'Micro', for example, is put before 'metre' to form 'micrometre' ($\mu$), whose value is $10^{-6}$, and 'giga' before 'byte' gives 'gigabyte' (G), whose value is $10^{9}$.

## Exponents

The exponent is the superscript number which denotes the power to which a number is multiplied, e.g. in $7^2$, the $^2$ is the exponent. Numbers are often expressed as powers of 10, such as $2.172 \times 10^5$ (= 217,200). This is called scientific notation and it makes arithmetic with large or small numbers much easier. For example, $2 \times 10 \times 10 \times 10 = 2 \times 10^3 = 2000$, or $3 \div 10 \div 10 \div 10 \div 10 = 3 \times 10^{-4} = 0.0003$.

Engineering notation is similar but uses powers of 10 in groups of three, such as $10^3$ or $10^{-9}$, corresponding to the SI prefixes. These prefixes make engineering notation neater when using very large or very small numbers, e.g. 5000 Hz = 5 kHz, or 0.000015 m = 5 $\mu$m.

---

## ▶ brilliant example

If you multiply a number by itself, this gives a positive power [n $\times$ n = 'n squared' = $n^2$ or 'n to the power 2'].

Dividing a number by itself gives that number to the power 0 and is equal to 1 [8/8 = $8^0$ = 1].

If you keep on dividing by the number, you get a negative power [$n^{-5} = 1/n^5$].

When you add numbers expressed as powers of 10, if the exponents are the same, you can add the numerical parts, but the exponent stays the same. [$(2.0 \times 10^{-3}) + (3.0 \times 10^{-3}) = 5.0 \times 10^{-3}$].

▶

If adding the numerical part produces a really large or small number, you might want to change the exponent [$(759 \times 10^5) + (605 \times 10^5) = 1364 \times 10^5 = 136.4 \times 10^6$].

If the numbers you're adding have different exponents, change them to the same power before adding the numerical parts [$(7.3 \times 10^4) + (6.0 \times 10^3) = (7.3 \times 10^4) + (0.6 \times 10^4) = 7.9 \times 10^4$].

When you're multiplying, add the exponents but multiply the numerical parts [$8 \times 10^5) \times (3 \times 10^4) = 24 \times 10^9$].

When you're using scientific notation to express large numbers, count up or down from the decimal point to work out what the exponent should be [$134.5 = 1.345 \times 10^2$ (count up two digits), $0.0029 = 2.0 \times 10^{-3}$ (count down three digits)].

To work out engineering notation more easily, group digits in threes from the decimal point, using commas [$15039829 = 15,039,829 = 15.04 \times 10^6$ to four significant figures, $0.000392 = 0.000,392 = 392 \times 10^{-6}$].

In both scientific and engineering notation, try to express the numeric part as a number between 0 and 1000 [rather than writing $0.1256 \times 10^6$, write $1.256 \times 10^5$ (scientific notation) or $125.6 \times 10^3$ (engineering notation)].

*Operators*

These are the mathematical signs which give instructions about what to do with variables and constants. We've already been using the basic ones: add ($+$), subtract ($-$), multiply ($\times$ or .), divide ($/$ or $\div$) and equals ($=$). There's also 'approximately equals' ($\approx$) and 'does not equal' ($\neq$). Frequently, the sign for 'multiply' is left out, so $mx$ means '$m$ multiplied by $x$'. The others you'll come across are 'greater than' ($>$), 'less than' ($<$), 'greater than or equal to' ($\geq$) and 'less than or equal to' ($\leq$). If your studies involve logs and powers, check the operators for them, too. In complex expressions or when there are mixed operations, it's important to carry them out in the right order. Use the mnemonic BODMAS, which shows the order you should use, moving from left to right – **b**rackets, powers **of**, **d**ivision, **m**ultiplication, **a**ddition, **s**ubtraction.

**brilliant** tip

The number zero produces specific, perhaps even strange effects. Multiply a number by zero and you get zero but divide a number or expression by zero and you get infinity. And that, mathematically, is meaningless.

## Equations

Numbers and symbols, which are usually letters, may be linked together in equations (formulae) or functions. They're a sort of shorthand which expresses the relationship between different quantities, or terms, and they're useful when you want to model, estimate or predict something. This is the branch of mathematics called algebra.

Equations are valuable because you can rearrange them to find the value of the various elements within them. For example, if you wanted to find a particular variable or constant in a formula, you could express it in terms of other variables and constants whose values you already know. It sounds complex but can be quite simple. Usually, you do it by making the same change on both sides of the equation which results in something disappearing from one side and reappearing on the other. For example, if you want to find the value of $y$ in the equation $x = y - z$, add $z$ to each side to give $x + z = y - z + z$, which means that $y = x + z$.

From that example, you can see that it can be a process of reduction – making things simpler and/or expressing them in a different mathematical way – so let's look at some other ways of manipulating numbers and equations.

- When you're working out results, do the calculations inside the brackets first, e.g. $(ab) + c \neq a(b + c)$ ; $(3 \times 5) + 6 \neq 3 \times (5 + 6)$ because $15 + 6 \neq 3 \times 11$.

- If there's a multiplying constant or variable, you can remove it by dividing both sides by it, e.g. if $x = yz$, then $y = x/z$ (divide both sides by $z$).

- If it's a dividing constant or variable, you multiply both sides by it, e.g. if $x = y/z$, then $y + xz$ (multiply both sides by $z$).

- Remove a power from one side by multiplying both sides by the reciprocal power, e.g. if $a = b^c$, then $b = a^{1/c}$.

- You can also achieve this by taking logs, e.g. if $a = b^c$, then $b = a^{1/c}$. If $a = b^c$, then $log\ a = c\ log\ b$, and $c = log\ a/log\ b = log(a - b)$.

- You can combine powers and powers of powers, e.g. $a^b + a^c = a^{(b+c)}$ and $a^b - a^c = a^{(b-c)}$. $(a^b)^c = a^{(bc)}$

- Before you do any of this manipulating, it's often useful to combine expressions or express them in different ways. Use parentheses ( ... ) to 'isolate' parts of formulae and calculations, as in $ab + ac = a(b + c)$. So, for example, if you wanted to find the value of $a$ in $y = ax + az$, change it to $y = a(x + z)$ before dividing both sides by $(x + z)$ to get $a = y/(x + z)$.

- You could use a similar technique to find $x$ in the equation $xy^2 - xz = 5 - p$. First 'isolate' $x$, which gives you $x(y^2 - z) = 5 - p$. Now divide both sides by $(y^2 - z)$ which leaves you with $x = (5 - p)/(y^2 - z)$.

## Logarithms ('logs')

A log to the base 10 is the power of 10 that would give that number. So $log\ (100) = 2$, because $10^2 = 10 \times 10 = 100$. In some situations, it's mathematically convenient to use natural logs (ln), which are powers of $e$ ($\approx 2.178$). Some examples will show how calculating with logs can simplify a task:

$$\log (a) \times \log (b) = \log (a + b)$$
$$\log (a) \div \log (b) = \log (a - b)$$
$$\log (a^n) = n \log (a)$$

You can convert a log value into a simple numerical value by working out its antilog, which is $10^x$, where $x$ is the log value. The equivalent for natural logs is $e^x$. If you want to get these values, it's better if you use a calculator.

Logs were very useful tools when people used to do complex calculations 'by hand' using old-fashioned mechanical calculators such as slide rules. Nowadays, the same jobs are made much easier by using digital calculators. But it's important for you to understand the mathematical origin of logs because you'll still find them in some formulae. For example, the degree of acidity, or pH, is calculated as $pH = -\log [H^+]$, where $[H^+]$ is the molar hydrogen ion concentration.

## Significant figures

Sometimes, especially when you're using a calculator, you get an answer which has lots of digits, for example 12.326024221867, and it's important for you to know how many of those digits or significant figures (s.f.) you need to quote in your answer. If you don't include them in the intermediate steps of your calculations, your final result could be way off the mark. On the other hand, if your final result contains too many digits, it could imply a level of accuracy that's misleading. For example, if your thermometer can only be read to the nearest half degree, it's wrong to refer to a temperature of 15.34°C.

You'll often be asked to express your results to a certain number of s.f. You can work out this number by counting digits starting from the left at the first non-zero digit. 12.326024221867 has 14 significant figures and would be expressed as 12.326 to five s.f. and 12.33 to four s.f.

*Rounding*

Deciding what the last digit is going to be is called rounding and you can round up or down. In the previous example, we changed 12.326 to 12.33. That's because the digits to the right of the last significant one were greater than 0.5. If they'd been less than 0.5, we'd have rounded them down – so 12.324 would have become 12.32. If the digit is exactly 0.5, you usually round down if the preceding digit is even and up if it's odd. So, to three significant figures, 15.65 becomes 15.6, while 15.75 becomes 15.8.

If you're asked to 'express your answer to *n* decimal places', it's easier but it may still involve rounding. If your calculator reads 60.466023, an answer to two decimal places would be 60.47.

---

**brilliant** example

As long as a number doesn't begin with a zero, the number of significant figures is equal to the number of digits.

94.8263 has six s.f.

If it does begin with one or more zeros, start counting the s.f. after the last leading zero.

0.0000465 has three s.f.

'Internal' zeros count as s.f.

0.00044304 has five s.f.

Don't count trailing zeros as s.f. in whole numbers.

2300 has two s.f.

If they come after a decimal point, however, trailing zeros do suggest a certain accuracy of measurement, so they're included in the count.

10.10 cm has four s.f.

The number of decimal places is the number of digits after the decimal point, rounded up or down as appropriate.

56.78478 to two decimal places is 56.78; 56.78478 to three decimal places is 56.785.

When your calculations have several values, use the one with the least number of significant figures to decide how many s.f. to use in your answer.

$12.232 - 9.2 = 3.0$ (not 3.032), $176 \times 1.573 = 276$ (not 276.848), but if you convert 1456 m to km, you get 1.456 km, not 1 or 1.5 km.

Always round after you've done a calculation, not before.

The area in $cm^2$ of a rectangular piece of carpet where the sides have been measured to the nearest mm as $1286 \times 1237$ would be 15,908 $cm^2$, not $129 \times 124$ cm $= 15,996$ $cm^2$.

If you're asked to work out an answer, but not told how many s.f. to use, make the answer as close as possible to the figure the instrument you've used could realistically measure.

Let's say you measure the length of a piece of string with a ruler and get 134 mm. When you convert millimetres to inches by multiplying 134 by 0.03937, your calculator will tell you it's 5.27558 inches, but your ruler couldn't possibly be that accurate, so you round the figure up to three s.f., i.e. 5.28 inches.

## Fractions

- A fraction is just one number divided by another. The number above the line is called the numerator, the one below it is the denominator.

- A common fraction involves two integer numbers (for example, 3/4).

- When the numerator is smaller than the denominator, the fraction represents a number between 0 and 1. When it's bigger, the fraction represents a number greater than 1.

- If you can divide both the numerator and the denominator by a common factor, you usually write it using the lowest possible values. 9 and 24 can both be divided by 3 so $^9/_{24} = {}^3/_8$.

- In a decimal fraction the denominator is always a factor of 10, such as $^3/_{10}$. These fractions are often written using the decimal point (for example $0.34 = {}^{34}/_{100}$).

## *Manipulating fractions*

When you're adding fractions, make sure the denominators are the same by multiplying both sides of one of the fractions by a number that makes this happen, then add the numerator values.

$^3/_4 + {}^1/_2 = ({}^3/_4 + {}^2/_4) = {}^5/_4 = 1{}^1/_4 = 1.25$ (We've multiplied both sides of the second fraction by 2 to express them both as fourths.)

In complex examples, you may need to multiply both sides of the fractions by different numbers. The object is to make all the denominators the same, in other words, you want to get the 'lowest common denominator'.

$^3/_8 + {}^2/_3 + {}^7/_9 = {}^{27}/_{72} + {}^{48}/_{72} + {}^{56}/_{72} = {}^{131}/_{72}$
(We've multiplied both sides of the first fraction by 9, the second's sides by 24 and the third's by 8 to get a lowest common denominator of 72.)

To multiply fractions, multiply both the numerators and denominators.

$^3/_4 \times {}^5/_2 = {}^{15}/_8$

The same applies for division. Divide both the numerators and denominators.

$^3/_4 \div {}^1/_2 = {}^3/_2$

Another way to divide is to turn the 'divided by' fraction round and multiply.

$$^3/_4 \div {}^1/_2 = {}^3/_4 \times {}^2/_1 = {}^6/_4 = {}^3/_2$$

### brilliant tip

It'll help if you memorise these common fractions as decimals (the $r$ indicates a repeating digit): $^1/_2 = 0.50$, $^1/_3 = 0.33r$, $^1/_8 = 0.125$, $^1/_4 = 0.25$, $^1/_5 = 0.20$, $^1/_{10} = 0.10$

## Percentages

- A percentage value is a fraction expressed as a number of hundredths.

- To calculate a common fraction as a percentage using a calculator, divide the numerator by the denominator and multiply the answer by 100: $^3/_4 = 0.75 = 75$ per cent = 75%.

- To convert a percentage into a decimal fraction, move the decimal point two places to the left.

- A percentage doesn't have to be a whole number: 65.34 per cent is valid. It doesn't always have to be less than 100 either. It's perfectly legitimate, for example, to say 'Jane earns 143 per cent of what John earns'.

- But if you're expressing a fraction of a limited total, you must stay within those limits, i.e, between 1 and 100. You can't, for example, say '126 per cent of dogs prefer Bonzo dog food'. Equally, those sports persons and others who claim to 'give 110 per cent' (or even more) clearly don't understand what percentages are.

*Manipulating percentages*

To work out one number as a percentage of another, divide the two and multiply by 100.

12 out of 76 as a percentage is: $^{12}/_{76} \times 100 = 16\%$ (That's 15.78947 rounded up.)

To find a percentage of a number, make the percentage a decimal fraction and multiply the number by it.

75% of 320 = 0.75 $\times$ 320 = 240

Don't get confused by percentages less than one.

0.05% is 5 in 10000 or $^{5}/_{10000}$

## Ratios

- A ratio expresses two or more numbers or portions in relation to each other, usually by dividing the larger by the smaller or, if there are more than two, dividing the others by the smallest.

- If you had 6 red, 12 blue and 36 orange discs, the ratio of red to blue to orange would be 1:2:6.

- Ratios can involve real numbers, such as 1.43:1.

- It may be easier to express ratios as decimal numbers in relation to unity. For example, if there are 34 girls in a class of 56, the ratio of girls to boys is $34/(56-34):1 = 1.5:1$ (rounded to one decimal place).

### brilliant dos and don'ts

**Do**

✔ get to know your calculator. Find out what kind of notation it uses (most use standard but there's also reverse-Polish) and how the memory works.

✔ learn how to do nested calculations, how to enter a constant and use it in several calculations, how to enter exponents and how to express one number as a percentage of another.

- express all values in formulae in terms of base units (i.e. metres, seconds, grams). Nearly all scientific and engineering formulae are expressed in terms of SI base units, so if you're given a length as 10 mm, don't enter it as 10, express the length in metres by entering $10 \times 10^{-3}$.

- check the units and scale of your answers. First, make sure that you convert them into the units the question asks for, and with the right number of s.f. Second, make sure your answer isn't absurdly high or low. Try to relate things such as areas and volumes to 'real life' by imagining, for example, what the value you've got might look like in relation to something you're familiar with, like a stamp, piece of paper, glass of beer, and so on.

- replace symbols with real numbers if you're unsure about using algebra correctly.

## What next?

### Check which mathematical skills ...

... you'll need to use in your research. You can probably judge this from the data collection techniques you'll be using and from your previous experience in practicals or lab work. Don't be afraid to ask your supervisor for guidance on this. Try some sample calculations to find out which areas you may need to revise.

### Learn, revise and practise ...

... all your mathematical skills. Decide which ones you feel less confident about and work on them. Start with the main principles and techniques in each topic, then move on to the ones which are specific to the type of work you'll be doing. You really need to understand the background well. Don't just rely on calculators and spreadsheets.

**If you're going to be doing ...**

... repeated calculations, set up some templates for them. It'll save you time. Create pre-formatted areas for data entry and presentation of results, with the relevant formulae already embedded in the spreadsheet. Pre-formatted graphical output may also be useful; even if you won't be using it in your report, you can refer to it to check measurements or experiments. Test your templates with data for which you know the answer, or can easily find it out.

**brilliant** recap

- Familiarise (or re-familiarise) yourself with basic numbers and symbols and mathematical processes.

- Understand the differences between constants, variables, units, prefixes, exponents and operators.

- Use equations and logarithms to make your calculations more manageable.

- Learn to use fractions, percentages and ratios.

**CHAPTER 16**

Working
with and
presenting
data

D ata, graphs, tables and statistics are all essential elements of many, maybe even most types of research. You'll need to be able to understand and interpret them as well as generate your own graphs and tables from raw data. This chapter offers reminders of the basics of data interpretation and gives hints on how to create your own graphs, charts and tables.

## Graphs, tables and basic statistics

The way data sets are presented can affect how you analyse them and may also push you toward a particular interpretation. So when you're examining graphs, tables and statistics, analyse them carefully and make sure the method you use to interpret them is sound. Also, when you create your own, try to condense and display your information in an unbiased way that makes it easy to understand.

> the way data sets are presented can affect how you analyse them

### brilliant tip

A quick way of finding out about different graph types is to explore a spreadsheet program like Microsoft Excel. The 'Insert > Chart > Standard Types' menu shows examples and gives brief descriptions of how they work. It'll also help you to decide the best way to present your own data.

## Reading graphs

There are several things which help to make it easier to read a graph and prevent it being misleading. Figure 16.1 identifies the basic components you're likely to find. If you use all the indicators carefully, you'll be less likely to misinterpret the information in it.

### Title and caption

These are usually below the graph. They tell you the subject of the graph and the particular aspects of it which are being shown. If the caption's quite detailed, you can come back to it later. It'll be easier to interpret after you've studied the graph itself.

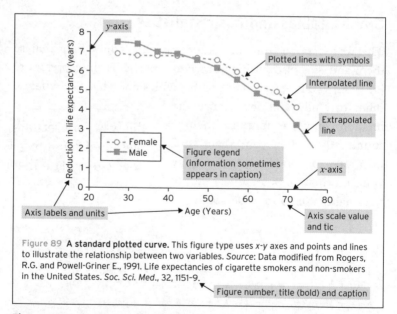

Figure 89 **A standard plotted curve.** This figure type uses *x*-*y* axes and points and lines to illustrate the relationship between two variables. *Source*: Data modified from Rogers, R.G. and Powell-Griner E., 1991. Life expectancies of cigarette smokers and non-smokers in the United States. *Soc. Sci. Med.*, 32, 1151–9.

**Figure 16.1** The basics of a graph

*Source*: McMillan & Weyers: *How to Write Dissertations and Project Reports*, Prentice Hall, 2010.

brilliant tip

The six basic steps for interpreting a graph are:

1  Read the title, legend and main text to check the context.

2  Note the type of graph.

3  Examine the axes.

4  Inspect their scale.

5  Study the symbols and curves to work out what's being plotted and where.

6  Work out the importance and significance of any error bars or statistics.

## Type of figure

The more charts and graphs you see, the more familiar you'll become with the various types. Figure 16.1 shows a basic plotted curve and Figure 16.2 has examples of (a) a pie chart, (b) a histogram and (c) a frequency polygon. The one you choose will depend on what you want to convey. A pic chart, for example, shows very clearly the comparative sizes of elements that go to make up an overall total; a histogram shows amounts in different categories and a frequency polygon shows the distribution of counted data across a continuous range.

## Axes

Very often, charts show the relationship between two variables, called $x$ and $y$ for convenience. The $x$-axis, which is a horizontal line along the bottom of the chart, usually measures the 'controlled' variable, which might be such things as age, time or distance. The $y$-axis, a vertical line to the left of the chart, relates to the 'measured' variable, for example income, weight, or life expectancy.

The same graph can measure more than one variable. If, for example, you were comparing the volume of sales for two or

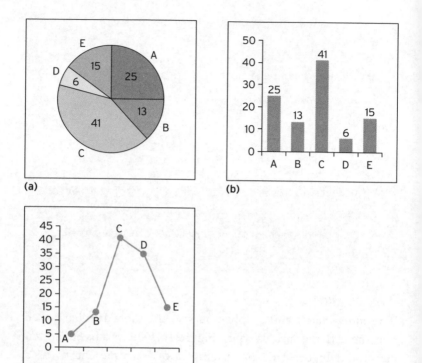

(a)

(b)

(c)

**Figure 16.2 Common types of graph.** You can use these as well
as the standard plotted curve shown in Figure 16.1. (a) **Pie chart**,
which shows breakdowns of a total – in this case they're percentages.
(b) **Histogram**, which shows the amounts in different categories. (c)
**Frequency polygon**, which shows the distribution of counted data
across a continuous range

*Source*: McMillan & Weyers: *How to Write Dissertations and Project Reports*, Prentice
Hall, 2010.

more products, the numbers sold would be on the *x*-axis, the period of time of the survey would be along the *y*-axis, and different coloured lines would be traced to plot the volume of sales of each product. The important thing is to choose the graph that best suits your aim.

## brilliant definition

Make sure you get these plurals right:

Axis = singular
Axes = plural
Datum = singular
Data = plural (the data *are* presented ...)

### Axis scale and units

A label on each axis should tell you what the axis represents and what units are being used (months, years, amounts and so on). The values are shown as a series of numbered cross-marks along the axis. Not all axes start from zero and some don't follow a straightforward linear progression. Sometimes, for example, if there's a particularly wide range of numbers to record, you'll see a logarithmic axis. You need to be careful when this happens because the graph might exaggerate or emphasise differences in a misleading way. To see what we mean, look at Figure 16.3 on the next page and note what happens when you change values on the *y*-axis in (a) and (b).

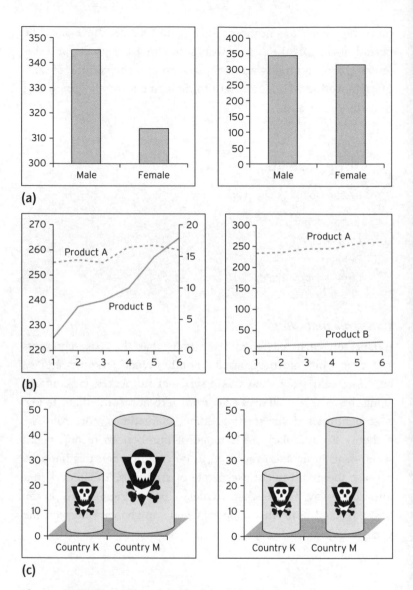

**Figure 16.3 Three examples of misleading graphs.**
**(a) A non-zero axis.** In the chart on the left, the y-axis starts at 300 and the differences between males and females seem large. Start at zero and they're less noticeable.
**(b) Different y-axes for different curves.** On the left, sales of product B (measured on the right-hand axis) seem to be overtaking those of product A (left axis). Using the same axis for both tells a different story.

**(c) Using a two- or three-dimensional object to represent a linear scale.** On the left, the barrel keeps its shape in relation to the y-axis scale, so M seems to produce much more toxic waste than K. The chart on the right is more accurate.

*Source*: McMillan & Weyers: *How to Write Dissertations and Project Reports*, Prentice Hall, 2010.

## Symbols and plotted curves

The symbols identify the different data sets on the chart and the curves suggest the relationship between the points in each one. There may be a legend or key to make this clearer. But this is where you need to be careful with your interpretations. If you're looking at the differences in the relationships, you'll obviously be using the plotted curves (also known as 'trend lines'), but the only truly accurate points on the curve are those which have been plotted. The lines joining them are usually hypothetical interpolations or, even less reliable, extrapolations which don't join two points but simply extend the line from a single one. Figure 16.1 identifies these features.

## Graphs can mislead

You can learn a lot about data presentation by reviewing misleading graphs and seeing why they might lead to incorrect interpretations. A selection of examples is shown in Figure 16.3. Don't use these forms of misrepresentation when you're constructing your own figures; you'll only confuse your readers.

### brilliant definition

Interpolation: an assumed trend or relationship between available data points. In simple terms, it's the line joining the plotted dots.

Extrapolation: an assumed trend or relationship before or after (below or above) available data points. This time it's a line drawn before the first or after the last plotted point. Extrapolation is risky because it's really a form of guesswork. It assumes a trend will continue without having any concrete evidence that it will.

## Creating graphs

If we could just give you a template to use, we would, but the reasons for using graphs are even more numerous than the types of graph available, so all we can do is give you some general pointers.

---

### ❓ brilliant questions and answers

**Q What's the graph for?**

**A** You have to decide why you need a graph and what you want it to do. That'll help you to choose the best type for the data you have. If you go for a plotted curve, think about which variable will be on the *x*- and which on the *y*-axis. If you choose a type you're not familiar with, do a rough sketch of how it'll present your data. You can use a spreadsheet to help you.

**Q What should the axes' range and units be? What are the upper and lower limits of your data? Should you start each axis at zero? If you don't, will it distort the presentation? (see Figure 16.3(a)) Will your axes be linear? Will they use the same units as your measurements, or will they be ratios, percentages or some other form?**

**A** These are all questions to answer before you start plotting the data in graph form. Once you've done that, write the label for the axis, saying what you're showing and then, in parentheses ( ) or after a solidus (/), the units you're using. Other types of graph, such as a pie chart, may need labels for each segment, or a legend or key.

---

### *Presentational choices*

You want it to be as clear and easy to read as possible so take some time choosing how you'll present the data. For pie charts, colour or shade the segments to make them distinct. If you're using axes, decide how frequently the tics should appear: too many will look crowded, too few will make it hard to work out the values of data points. Choose clear symbols for each set of data and, if you have a sequence of graphs, keep the symbols consistent.

take some time choosing how you'll present the data

**brilliant** tip

If you're adding a curve to a graph, be careful with it. By linking different plotted points, you're assuming and implying that there's a relationship between them. It's rare for these points to be completely free of error, so your curve should take an 'average' line between them.

## Captions

It's best if your figure is 'self-contained'; in other words, it should have everything the reader needs to understand it without having to look for extra information elsewhere. Your caption should carry:

- the number and title of the figure (Figure 16.1 The basic components of a graph, Figure 16.2 Common forms of graph, etc.);
- an indication of what the symbols and error bars mean;
- if appropriate, how the plotted curve was chosen;
- any brief details about the data that will help to make it clearer.

## Creating tables

Normally, you wouldn't include the same data in a chart and a table, so which should you use? Well, in general, a table would be better if:

- some or all of your data aren't suitable for presentation in graphic form (for instance, when some are qualitative);
- there are too many data sets or variables to put in a chart;
- your reader might want to know the exact values of some of your data;
- you want to include large amounts of your data (for instance in an appendix to a report).

Remember:

Quantitative data – data that can be expressed in numbers, such as length, height or price.

Qualitative data – data that are descriptive and non-numerical, such as colour, place of manufacture, or name.

Before you start on the final version of your table, think about it and draw a rough design to make sure it has everything you need.

### Titles and captions

Just as with graphs, you need to add these to tell the reader what the table's about. They should always be above the table. Also, they're numbered independently from graphs, so as well as Figure 16.1, you'll have Table 16.1.

## Columns, rows and headings

Each column should display a particular type of data which you should describe clearly in the heading. If the data are quantitative, include the units too. The rows will show different instances of the various types of data. To take a simple example, if you were compiling a table to compare responses to a questionnaire about education, the columns might be headed 'Teachers', 'Parents', 'Educationalists', 'Pupils' while the rows could indicate attitudes to 'Discipline', 'Range of subjects', 'Length of school day' and so on.

When you create a table using Word, the default offers you a set of enclosed boxes but nowadays the tendency is to use just horizontal lines.

### Data values

You should give these to an appropriate number of significant figures. If you want to include an indication of errors, put this in brackets and make it clear in the heading what statistic you're quoting. If you need to explain any abbreviations or give details of specific cases, you can add them in footnotes.

## Statistics and testing hypotheses

You can use statistics to test a hypothesis by comparing the properties of a data set with other samples or with some theory about it. First, let's note that all data sets carry degrees of error and variability in their values.

- Sampling errors arise when only a few individuals are chosen from a large, variable population.
- Measurement errors result from how the variable is measured.
- You get rounding errors when you reduce findings to an appropriate number of significant figures and then use them in calculations, which increases the level of error.
- Human errors include writing or copying data inaccurately, mixing up of samples, and many more.
- There are also miscellaneous errors whose origins are difficult to identify or result from other sampling effects.

So it's impossible to be 100 per cent certain about differences between sets. They may be 'genuine' and show that there really is a dissimilarity between the samples, perhaps because of something you've done to one of them. On the other hand, the differences may just be the result of random errors. Hypothesis testing works by looking at these alternatives and deciding which is most likely to be true.

The usual approach is to set up a 'null hypothesis' (NH) that says that the samples are the same or that they both match some theoretical description. You can then make certain assumptions about the data and calculate a statistic to test the hypothesis. You can then use calculations or tables of probability to find how likely it is that the NH is true. The lower the probability, the less chance there is that it's correct. Generally speaking, if the probability is less than 0.05, you reject the NH.

## brilliant dos and don'ts

### Do

✔ learn how to use spreadsheets to create charts. Most of the simpler functions are easy to use but you may want to change some of the elements and that might need some advanced knowledge of the program. If you're uncertain about it, get someone to help you.

✔ learn the table functions in your word processor. You'll produce more presentable and user-friendly tables if you're familiar with the techniques of adding and deleting columns and rows, manipulating their widths, adding and removing cell borders, merging and splitting cells and sorting data.

✔ some research on statistics. Some of the terminology involved can often make them seem hard to understand but, as with most things, practice will make them easier. If you're not entirely confident about your ability to handle them, it might be worth doing a supplementary module or buying extra texts to help you improve.

### Don't

✘ accept the default values offered by spreadsheets without checking to see whether they really do suit your purposes. Scale, background, gridlines, symbols, lines and other aspects can all be changed.

## What next?

### Analyse graphs ...

... produced by different people. You'll see that graphs in newspapers, for example, often tend to be presented in a way that supports the journalist's viewpoint, while those in academic articles are less likely to show such bias because they're peer-reviewed. Whatever type you're looking at, think about why its creator chose that particular format, whether it helps you to understand the issues and how it could be improved.

**Find out how tables ...**

... are normally presented in your discipline. We've talked about the possible variations – cell borders, lines, size of cells and so on – so you do have choices. But you'll probably be expected to use the same style as the one you see in text and journal articles in your area. If in doubt, ask a colleague or your supervisor.

**brilliant** recap

- Learn how to 'read' a graph and make your own graphs easy to interpret.
- Understand the elements of which the graph is composed.
- Study the different types of graph and choose the one best suited to displaying your data.
- Understand the functions of the constituent parts of tables and create tables which are easy to read.
- Use statistics to test your hypothesis.

# PART 6

# Plagiarism, referencing and ethics

**CHAPTER 17**

# Never ever plagiarise

Plagiarism and copyright are two related topics that are extremely important academically and legally. They may seem complex at times and they're often misunderstood by students. Dissertations and project reports tend to use more citations than simpler types of academic writing because of their length, structure and depth. You therefore need to be fully aware of the issues involved. If you don't find out what these terms mean and how they could affect your university career, you could be risking serious disciplinary action.

## Plagiarism is stealing

If you take someone else's ideas and pretend they belong to you, that's theft, plain and simple. The problem is that over recent years technological advances such as digital scanners, photocopiers and file-sharing have all made it much easier to cut, copy and paste things. You may even do so without knowing you're doing it. So it really is in your interests to get to know exactly when and how you need to acknowledge intellectual property. Apart from anything else, wouldn't you rather develop your own ideas than steal other people's? Isn't that why you're at university?

> if you take someone else's ideas and pretend they belong to you, that's theft

## brilliant definition

**Plagiarism** – using the work of someone else as if it were your own without acknowledging the source. (Note. 'Work' here includes ideas, writing and inventions – not just words.)

Intentional plagiarism is a very serious offence. Universities impose a range of penalties depending on how severe the case is. It may just be a reduction in marks or it could be exclusion from the university or a refusal to give you a degree. You'll find the sanctions imposed by your own institution in your departmental or school handbook.

With such severe consequences, it's hard to believe anyone would still deliberately set out to cheat in this way. But part of the problem is that you may be plagiarising without knowing you're doing it. It's the sort of thing that happens when you've read something a while ago and actually forgotten you've read it. Then, as you're thinking about your subject, some ideas come into your head which you assume to be yours whereas in fact they're memories of your original reading. The best way of avoiding this is to be scrupulous about noting down full details of each source as you consult it.

You can, of course, use other people's ideas and words; in fact, it's good academic practice to do so. But you must always acknowledge the source. If you think an author has said something particularly well, quote her directly and provide a reference to the relevant article or book beside the quote. The academic convention for direct quotes is to use inverted commas (and sometimes italics) to identify it as original material taken directly from a source.

**brilliant** tip

We're not just talking about stealing from books and articles. Copying a friend's or a classmate's work is cheating, too. And both people involved may be punished for it. If you let someone copy your work, you're as guilty as he is. So if you're tempted to be Mr Nice Guy and 'help out' someone else in this way, resist. It's not worth the risk.

## Cutting and pasting

It's plagiarism if you cut or copy something from a source such as a website, for example, and paste it into your own work without citing it. There are very sophisticated programs now which can scan a text and identify sections which have been copied from elsewhere. More and more, universities and departments are using them to eliminate such practices.

> sophisticated programs can identify sections copied from elsewhere

**brilliant** example

**Danny the plagiarist**

Danny uses material direct from the source without any acknowledgement. It's blatant plagiarism.

The source reads: Most accidents are alcohol-related: 50% are fatalities but not necessarily of those under alcoholic influence (Annual Police Statistics, 2004; in Milne, 2006).

Danny's version is: The majority of road accidents are alcohol-related and 50% of these cases result in a death, but not always of the person who has consumed the alcohol.

▶

All he's done is rearrange the order slightly without noting the source. On top of that, by not saying where he got them, the 'facts' might just as well be guesswork. A better version would be: A study of police statistics by Milne (2006) reported that approximately half of road accidents result in a death because one of the parties involved has been under the influence of alcohol.

### Stella the word-shifter

Stella thinks that, if she just changes odd words and the word order of the original, she's not plagiarising. She's wrong.

The source states: 'Post-operative physiotherapy is vital to the improvement in the quality of life of the elderly patient' (Kay, 2003).

Stella writes: Therapy after surgery is critical to the recovery of the older patient and their quality of life (Kay, 2003).

She's simply used a couple of synonyms and reversed two points, which doesn't really show that she's understood it.

An alternative version might be: Kay (2003) attributes the improved quality of life levels of elderly patients who have undergone surgery to physiotherapy treatment. (Using the verb 'attributes' shows that it's Kay's claim, but that the person reporting it doesn't necessarily agree with it.)

### Eileen and the missing marks

When Eileen quotes the exact words from the original text, she makes sure she cites the source. The problem is that she forgets to put in the quotation marks. And that's plagiarism.

The original is: It could be assumed that undergraduate students wrote what they could write and not what they actually know.

Eileen's version reads: Sim (2006) asserted that students wrote what they could write and not what they actually know.

She's cited the source, but hasn't used the punctuation marks to isolate the words she's 'borrowed'. A more correct version would be: Sim (2006) asserted that students 'wrote what they could write and not what they actually know'.

## Ed and the missing citations

Ed and Eileen should get together because he's guilty of the opposite omission. He copies words from the original text, puts them inside quotation marks, then forgets to source the quotes. It's yet another form of plagiarism.

Ed's version of the same source material as Eileen used is: Essentially, what was noted was that the students 'wrote what they could write and not what they actually know'. All it needs is the simple (Sim 2006) at the end or, alternatively, to insert it at the beginning, i.e. Sim (2006) noted that students 'wrote what they could write and not what they actually know'.

## Sally's strings of sources

Sally's having trouble understanding her subject and isn't confident about her own writing. She reads lots, picks out the bits she thinks are relevant, and strings them together. She's careful to add the sources and hopes that this proof that she's read widely will show she understands the subject. It's bad academic practice, creates text that's hard to read and doesn't convince the reader that she knows what she's writing about. It could also be considered to be plagiarism. Here's a typical paragraph.

> Brown (2000) noted 'insomnia is the ailment of the elderly'. Smith (2004) stated 'insomnia is a function of stressful living'. Jones (2001) said 'insomnia is a figment of those who sleep for an average of five hours a night'. This means that insomnia is a problem.

It's just a sort of shopping list of sources and she's made no connections between them. She's also failed to see that Jones's comment is different from the others in that it suggests that those who claim insomnia don't actually suffer from it. How much better it would have been if she'd linked the ideas, e.g. Perceptions about the incidence of insomnia are varied. Insomnia is problematic for the elderly (Brown, 2000) and for the stressed (Smith, 2004). However, Jones (2001) contends that people who claim to be insomniacs actually sleep for an average of five hours per night. This suggests that insomnia is often a perception rather than a reality.

▶

### Jeff the downloader

Jeff has done the prescribed reading and produced a piece of text. But there are problems. When compared with the rest of what he's written it seems too good, too fluent. It also contains hypertext links and there's no citation. It's an obvious example of internet plagiarism. Here's what he wrote.

> The incidence of drug misuse is something that invites action from international agencies including the WHO. There are also European organisations that have recognised the need to counter drug trafficking as well as establishing drug rehabilitation regimens throughout the European theatre.

He hasn't bothered to rework the material – it's just a straight steal. It also shows that he's content to rely on a source that may not have been monitored or authenticated and failed to consult literature from more academic sources. It would have been so much easier to simply write: International and European organisations have engaged in tackling drug trafficking, misuse, and rehabilitation. (www.drugfree.org accessed 1.1.07)

### Marie and Tim the sharers

Marie has worked closely with her student buddy, Tim. They've shared material and they've both used the same diagram in their work without saying how it originated. Marie wrote 'Figure 3 shows that … (diagram inserted)' while Tim wrote 'Figure 3 illustrates that … (diagram inserted)'.

The diagram was the product of their collaboration but, paradoxically, they're both guilty of plagiarism. It's good to work with a buddy to discuss and sketch a diagram but, for the final version, they should have worked independently. They should then acknowledge the contribution of their partner either in the text, the figure legend, the acknowledgements, or the reference list.

## Good paraphrasing

If all you do is change an odd word or reconfigure the order of the words in the original, that's very close to plagiarism. Good paraphrasing shows that you understand the concepts and ideas of the original text – in fact it proves that you're capable of critical thinking. It also gives your reader a broad idea of the key points or arguments without having to read all the source material. What you're doing is freely rewriting the original, retaining its meaning and possibly adding extra points.

## The importance of copyright

When you see the copyright symbol © it tells you that someone is making it clear that the words you're reading and the ideas they're expressing belong to them. But just because you don't see any such symbol, it doesn't mean that anyone can quote it without acknowledging the source. The material may still be copyright. We're dealing here with a highly complex legal situation and what we say can give only general indications of what's involved.

Nonetheless, it's important for you to be aware of the nature of copyright and avoid infringing it. Once again, that is stealing. Under the law, your work is protected and others can't use it without your permission. In the UK, that protection applies during the author's lifetime and for 70 years afterwards. That's why you usually see © accompanied by a date and the owner's name at the start of a book.

> be aware of the nature of copyright and avoid infringing it. Once again, that is stealing

So you need to be sure that you're not breaking the law when you're photocopying something, digitally scanning it or printing it out without the owner's permission. This isn't as harsh as it sounds because educational copying, for non-commercial private study or research, is usually allowed by publishers. But it's better to stay safe and make sure you copy only a small amount of material under what's called the 'fair dealing' provision. There's no precise legal definition for this but it means just using very short extracts and acknowledging the source.

> ### brilliant tip
>
> The laws as we're describing them apply to what's classified as 'private study or research' and that means exactly what it says. If you're using the material for commercial or other reasons, such as photocopying a funny article for your friends, that's illegal. So is copying software and music CDs (including 'sharing' MP3 files).

## How much can you copy?

It's safer to ask at your library or in your department to find out exactly how much you can copy and what the general copying rules are. In general, you shouldn't copy more than 5 per cent of the work involved, or:

- one chapter of a book;
- one article per volume of an academic journal;
- 20 per cent (to a maximum of 20 pages) of a short book;
- one poem or short story (maximum of 10 pages) from an anthology;
- one separate illustration or map up to A4 size;
- short excerpts of musical works – not whole works or movements.

In each of these cases we're talking about single copies. You're not allowed to make multiple copies of any of these or hand over a single copy for multiple copying to someone else.

Even if you're copying from something you bought and which you therefore own, such as a book or CD, if you copy it or a significant part of it without permission, you're infringing copyright.

And the same rules apply to text, music and/or images on the internet. Some sites do offer copyright-free images but you should check the home page to see if there's a statement about copyright or a link to one.

## brilliant dos and don'ts

### Do

✔ make sure you always quote the source when you're copying material by electronic means. It's only too easy to highlight some text, then copy and paste it into a file and move on. If you then use it in your work without saying where you got it, you could be in trouble.

✔ write full details of sources when you're making notes. Do this on the same piece of paper that you used to summarise them or copy them out. And when you take down phrases and extracts using the exact words of the original, always put quote marks around them. When you look at them later, you may not remember that they're direct quotes and it's important to acknowledge that they are in any material you submit. You may not use them in your final draft but even if you just paraphrase them, you still have to cite the source.

✔ double-check all your 'original' ideas. Your individual take on a subject may represent a fresh, unique insight into a topic but, equally, it may be something you read months before which has just resurfaced. Think carefully about possible sources and, if you're not sure, check with people such as your tutor or supervisor to see whether the idea's familiar to them, or look at relevant texts, encyclopaedias or the internet.

### Don't

✘ paraphrase a source too closely; if all you're doing is taking key phrases and rearranging them, or just replacing some words with synonyms, that's still plagiarism.

▶

✗    use too many quotations. A text which simply strings together
chunks of other people's ideas will probably make for dull,
uneven reading and will certainly be guilty of plagiarising.

## What next?

### Double-check your department's ...

... (or university's) plagiarism policy. This should tell you what
the rules are and how you might break them. It'll also give you
information on how to cite sources.

### Read the notices in the library ...

... about photocopying or, if there aren't any, ask about it.

### When you're making notes ...

... highlight and put quotations marks around all direct tran-
scriptions. And (yes, we're saying it again) add full details of the
source whenever you take notes from a textbook or other paper
source.

### brilliant recap

- There are many forms of plagiarism. You must be fully aware
  of the issues involved.

- Avoid plagiarising by using good paraphrasing and
  summarising, and using quotations properly.

- Make sure you understand and respect the complexities of
  copyright. Don't break the rules.

# CHAPTER 18

# Citations and references

D rawing on the work of others is fundamental to all types of academic research and, as with all aspects of academic writing, there are formal rules to follow when it comes to acknowledging your sources. The particular referencing style you have to use in your own work will depend on your university's preferred option. But you'll need to be aware of how other systems operate so that you can understand references in the work of others. We'll take an overview of them here and outline the four main ones and how to use them.

## Acknowledging the work of others

Every kind of academic paper, from essays through project reports and dissertations to theses, refers to work done on the topic by others in the past. It's normal – in fact, it's essential – to read widely on your topic and benefit from what others have discovered or proposed. And, whether you quote directly from their texts or simply paraphrase their ideas, you must tell your reader exactly where you found the material so that she can locate your source for herself. So you do two things:

> you must tell your reader exactly where you found the material

1 indicate the source in the body of your text at the point where you refer to or quote it;

2    give full details of it in a footnote, endnote or separate
reference list at the end of your paper.

**brilliant** definition

**Citation** – details of the author and publication of an idea included
directly or indirectly in a text to show where it came from.

**Bibliography** – a listing at the end of your work of all the source
materials you've consulted. You don't need to have used them all
directly in your text.

**Reference list** – all the books, journals, web and online materials
you've referred to in your paper. It's usually placed at the end.

## Referencing styles

You'll find your department's preferred style in your course
handbook, or it may be recommended by your lecturer or supervisor. If there's no stated preference, the choice is yours, so you
need to have an idea of the sort of variations there are. That's
why we'll now look at the four most popular styles and highlight
how they work. To make it all simpler, we'll invent a book, its
author, publication date and publishers. Let's be pretentious and
call it *The existential lay-by* by K. J. Shiels, published by Pekinese
Press, Cambridge in 2007. None of the 'quotations' from it is
intended to be accurate or even to make much sense; they're
only there to provide examples of how citations and quotations
work.

When it comes to how you format the source for inclusion
in your reference list or bibliography, however, there are so
many possible variations (multiple authors, articles in newspapers, journals or in collections edited by someone else, online
resources, broadcasts and so on), that it would be confusing to
list them all here. Instead, we suggest that, once you know which

style your university prefers, you use a search engine to consult one of the many excellent sites which lay out examples of each very clearly. The search term Harvard style, Vancouver style, etc. is all you need.

## Harvard

This is maybe the simplest, quickest and possibly the easiest to adjust of the four.

- When you refer to the source in your text, you put the author's name and the date in brackets at the end of the sentence, e.g. Not all philosophies are sensible (Shiels, 2007). Note that this isn't a direct quote from Shiels but a paraphrase of his viewpoint.

- You can also make the author's name part of your sentence, putting the date in brackets immediately after it, e.g. Shiels (2007) argues that existentialism and absurdism occupy different points on the spectrum of despair.

- If you quote directly from the book, you must also add the relevant page number, e.g According to Shiels (2007, p. 23) 'dialectical materialism predicated a linear narrative which has today been undermined by the phenomenon of hypertext'.

- The way to identify the book in your reference list or bibliography is: Shiels, K. J., 2007. *The existential lay-by*. Cambridge: Pekinese Press. (Note. Everything, including the punctuation marks, must follow this exact pattern. The same applies with every other referencing style.)

## Modern Languages Association (MLA)

- When you refer to the source in your text, you put the author's name and the page number in brackets, e.g. Not all philosophies are sensible (Shiels, 126).

- You can also make the author's name part of your sentence, putting the page number in brackets at the end of the sentence or clause, e.g. Shiels argues that existentialism and absurdism occupy different points on the spectrum of despair (79).

- If you quote directly from the book, you must put the name and page number at the end of the sentence e.g. 'dialectical materialism predicated a linear narrative which has today been undermined by the phenomenon of hypertext' (Shiels 23).

- The way to identify the book in your reference list or bibliography is: Shiels, K. J. *The existential lay-by.* Cambridge: Pekinese Press, 2007.

## *Vancouver*

This is a numerical system with full-size numerals in brackets after the citation or quotation. Each number refers to a work listed in the bibliography or reference list, where the sources themselves are numbered 1, 2, 3, etc. It makes the text easier to read because there are no names or other bits of information interrupting the flow. On the other hand, if the reader wants to know the source of the reference, he has to stop reading and turn to the bibliography to find it. If you cite or quote more than once from a particular source, each time you put the same number in brackets, so if you're quoting from Shiels and two other imaginary writers, Ebeneezer Black and Billabong White, and the quotations/citations come in the order Black, Shiels, Shiels, White, Black, White, Shiels, the sequence of numbers in brackets will be (1), (2), (2), (3), (1), (3), (2).

The way to identify the book in your reference list or bibliography is:

Shiels K. J. The existential lay-by. Cambridge: Pekinese Press; 2007.

*Chicago*

This style uses footnotes. The first time a particular source is cited or quoted, the full bibliographical information is given in a footnote. Each time it's used after that, abbreviations are used. The sequence might be as follows:

- Shiels claimed that not all philosophies are sensible[1].
  The footnote will read:
  > [1] K. J. Shiels, *The existential lay-by*. (Cambridge: Pekinese Press, 2007), 126. (This means the reference is to page 126.)

- We'll assume that you're quoting or citing from other references and that they take up footnotes 2, 3 and 4, so the next time Shiels is sourced, the footnote will read:
  > [5] Shiels, *op. cit.*, 27 (*op. cit.* means 'work already quoted' and 27 is the page number).

- If there are no other references between this and the next Shiels one, the footnote will read:
  > [6] Shiels, *ibid.*, 159. (*Ibid* is short for *ibidem*, meaning 'the same'. It's indicating that it's the same Shiels text you've already quoted but this time the reference is to page 159.)

- The way to identify the book in your reference list or bibliography is: Shiels, K. J. 2007. *The existential lay-by*. Cambridge: Pekinese Press. (Notice that the layout of the full bibliographical information is formatted differently here compared with the footnote.)

## What's it all for?

This may seem fussy but there are good reasons for giving full information about the quotations and citations you use.

Ideas in books and articles belong to the people who express them. They themselves may have got them from others but if you're using their version, you must acknowledge that you're borrowing from them. Even if your aim is to disagree with them, you must still give them credit for what is their intellectual property.

> ideas in books and articles belong to the people who express them

Noting what sources you used will help your reader to understand how you put your own argument together and where it fits into general studies of and opinions about the topic. By knowing the sort of influences you responded to, he'll be better able to place your work and form opinions about it. It will also show him how much reading you've done and the scope of your knowledge of the subject. This will be useful if he's assessing your work or advising you on further reading or sources that are more relevant.

Finally, it'll give him the information he needs if he wants to read the source material for himself.

## brilliant tip

If you have a quotation contained inside another one, in British English you put the whole quotation in single inverted commas and the contained quotation in double inverted commas. To demonstrate this, here's another quote from our fictional author Shiels: 'Philosophy consists of more than Shakespeare's notion that "There's nothing either good or bad but thinking makes it so" but the words are a valuable starting point'. In American English, that becomes: "Philosophy consists of more than Shakespeare's notion that 'There's nothing either good or bad but thinking makes it so' but the words are a valuable starting point".

## Using information within your text

There are two ways of introducing the work of others into your text: by quoting exact words from a source; or by citation, which involves summarising or paraphrasing the idea in your own words. Remember that, in both cases, you must acknowledge the source of the material.

## Quotations

In this case, it depends whether the quotation's short or long. If it's short, put the exact words in single inverted commas within your own sentence. If we make xxxx your words and zzz the words of the quotation, this gives us: xxxx xx xxxx 'zzzz zz zzzz zz zzzz' xxx xxxx x xxx. If it's a long quotation, say 30 words or more, you don't use inverted commas. Instead, you separate it from your own text by indenting it and using single-spacing for it, like this:

Xxx xxxx x xxx xxxxxxxxx xxxxxxx xxxxx xxxx:

> Zzzz zz zzzzzz z zzzz zz zzzzzz zz zzzz zzzz zzzzz zz zzz zzzzzzzzzzzzzz zz zzzzz zzzzz zzzzzzz zzzzzzz zzzzz zz zz z zzzzzz z zz zzzzzzzz zzzz zz zzzzzzzz zzzzzzzzzzzzz zzz zzzzzzzzzzz (source reference)

Xxx xxxx x xxx xxxxxxxxx xxxxxxx xxxxx xxxx

If you deliberately miss out some words from the original, you show you've done so by filling the 'gap' with three dots. This is called ellipsis. For example, if the quotation in the last example started somewhere other than at the beginning of a sentence, you'd write:

Xxx xxxx x xxx xxxxxxxxx xxxxxxx xxxxx xxxx:

> ... zzz zz zzzzzz z zzzz zz zzzzzz zz zzzz zzzz zzzzz zz zzz zzzzzzzzzzzzzz zz zzzzz zzzzz zzzzzzz zzzzzzz zzzzz zz zz z zzzzzz z zz zzzzzzzz zzzz zz zzzzzzzz zzzzzzzzzzzzz zzz zzzzzzzzzzz (source reference)

Xxxxx xxx x xxx xxxxxxxxx xxxxxxx xxxxx xxxx

If the words are left out of the body of the quotation, ellipsis is still used but it's enclosed by square brackets to show that there wasn't an ellipsis in the original, e.g. 'zzz zz zzzzzz z zzzz zz zzzzzz [...] zzzz zzzz zzzzz zz zzz'.

> ### ☀ brilliant tip
>
> Cutting words out of a quote which aren't relevant to the point it's supporting helps to keep it brief and focused. But you must never omit words that change the sense of the quotation. If the quotation was 'The prospect of entry into a federal European Union is not universally acceptable', leaving out the word 'not' would change its meaning completely and misrepresent the views of the author.

### Formulae

You can include short formulae or equations in your text if you like but it's probably better to put them on a separate line and indent them like this:

$$\alpha + 4\beta / \eta^2 \, \pi = 0$$

That makes it easier for the reader.

### Citations

There are two basic ways of citing text: one stresses the information, while the other stresses the author. If we use the Harvard method for identifying the sources, examples of the two methods would be:

- Philosophical advances are almost entirely dependent on linguistic evolution (Shiels, 2007).
- Shiels (2007) claimed that philosophical advances were almost entirely dependent on linguistic evolution.

In the first, the statement reads as if it's a generally accepted 'truth' which he's articulating; in the second, it may still be a 'truth' but by putting the author at the beginning, it makes it seem more like his opinion.

## Footnotes and endnotes

In some disciplines, footnotes and endnotes identify the source of information, giving author, title, page number. More generally, they're used to provide additional information or add a comment or discussion point which would interrupt the flow of the argument if it was included in the text. Footnotes are at the bottom of the page on which the link appears. Endnotes are collected together at the end of the whole text.

### brilliant tip

In the examples in this chapter, we used the words 'argues' and 'claimed' to introduce quotations and/or citations from Shiels. There are lots of verbs that can be used in the same context, i.e. to report the views of others.

Some of the ones most frequently seen are:

| | | | |
|---|---|---|---|
| allege | contend | judge | show |
| assert | declare | note | state |
| claim | demonstrate | propose | suggest |
| consider | explain | report | warn |

They don't all mean the same thing, of course, and some are definitely 'stronger' than others. Choose carefully so that it's clear what you think the impact of the quoted or cited work is.

## Software referencing packages

These are flexible programs and can create your reference list in several different formats. But, unless you're very familiar with them, does it really make sense to spend time learning how to use such complex tools and keying in the data to 'feed' them? It would probably be quicker and produce the same results if you typed a list straight into a word-processed table and sorted it alphabetically.

## Making citing and listing references easier for yourself

It must be obvious by now that citations and quotations are crucial to the production of good quality academic writing. So get into good habits from the start. Whichever way you prefer to make and copy notes – electronically, photocopying, writing – make sure you always include all the necessary bibliographical information. If you don't, it'll take ages to find it later.

Choose or find out which reference style to use as early as possible. Don't switch between systems. Whichever you choose, follow its conventions to the letter, including all punctuation details. Once you've done so, add works to your reference list as you read them. Just set up a table or list and type in the relevant details as soon as you cite the source in the text. Using a table like this makes the formatting easier and lets you insert new records very easily.

Even if you're not sure whether you'll use a quotation you're noting down, you should still record full reference details with it. You may have an excellent memory but it'll still take time to locate the source and note down its details later. And if your memory's not so good, it'll be a very frustrating process.

# What next?

### Find out which referencing style ...

... is recommended for your subjects. These may be different from one subject to another. If you're not sure which you should be using, ask your supervisor or look at the way the referencing has been done in the books on your reading lists. You could also look at a well-known journal in your field to see what style it uses. You often find details in sections of a journal with a heading such as 'Guidelines for contributors'. If you compare it with the examples we've given, that should help you to identify the style by name.

## Look at textbooks or journal articles ...

... in your subject area to see what method they use for quotations. Sometimes direct quotations are common but sometimes they're rare and you need to know which applies in your subject.

## Check to see whether ...

... any software referencing packages are available in your university's electronic systems. Your library adviser or someone from IT support will probably be able to tell you how to use them. They could be useful if you know that your work has to be presented in one format for your dissertation or project report but may need to be changed to another in order to be submitted for publication to a learned journal. Most software referencing packages can translate between styles.

## brilliant recap

- Acknowledge your sources by referencing them correctly.

- There are four main academic styles: Harvard, MLA, Vancouver and Chicago. Understand the importance of using them.

- Know the difference between quotations and citations and how to use them.

- Make citing and listing references easy for yourself by getting into good habits.

# CHAPTER 19

# The ethical dimension

The word 'ethics' can extend to cover a wide spectrum of activities and behaviours. In the context of research, it refers to the way you carry out your investigation and implies that you must be careful to treat your subjects, human or otherwise, with respect and consideration. All research should make the health and safety of all those involved as participants or researchers a priority at all times. If you're in any doubt about your own department's or institution's ethical policies and practices, find out about them. Here, we'll just look at the general considerations and highlight the sort of things you should be aware of.

## Good research practice

You must get to know the ethical codes that apply in your area and that should be part of the initial discussion you have with your supervisor about how you're going to approach your project. She'll be responsible for making sure that your proposal meets the required standards in all its aspects. If necessary, she'll help you to prepare an application to send to your institution's ethics committee.

> you must get to know the ethical codes that apply in your area

## Ethical principles

If your research involves human beings, it must protect the human rights, dignity, health and safety of participants and researchers. In simple terms, this means that:

- it should do no harm;
- consent should be voluntary; and
- confidentiality should be respected throughout.

But even if there are no humans involved, there may still be ethical issues to resolve and in widely differing areas. For example, the use of animals, cloning, human embryo research, stem cell research, *in vitro* fertilisation and nuclear research all have clear ethical dimensions and have provoked lots of controversy. In the UK, experiments involving animals are subject to Home Office approval, and any research involving genetic manipulation must comply with the relevant legislation. As with all other aspects of your work, if this applies to you, your supervisor will guide you through the relevant procedures.

## Ethics committees

The members of these committees are academics from your institution and they monitor research activity at undergraduate and postgraduate levels. Their main functions are to:

- consider and approve applications to carry out research;
- hear appeals when approval hasn't been granted;
- give guidance on cases that aren't clear;
- refer cases of research misconduct to a higher institutional authority.

When the appropriate ethics committee has approved your work, you must follow its approved protocols exactly and if you modify your original proposal in any way, you have to resubmit it to them.

**brilliant** tip

If any aspect of your work involves risks such as exposure to hazardous chemicals, it'll be covered by policies and procedures set up by your university's safety office and may involve some paperwork on your part. So if you have to fill in forms such as those relating to the Control of Substances Hazardous to Health (COSHH), don't think of it as a chore. In fact, it's an opportunity for you to look at your topic from a different angle and get another perspective on what you're about to take on.

## Consent and confidentiality

You may have to inform people who agree to take part in your research about the things it may involve. If so, you'll need to give them a 'Participant Information Sheet'. The information on it should be comprehensive and contain:

- an outline of the purpose of the study;
- the invitation to take part and the reason they've been selected;
- an acknowledgement that they're taking part voluntarily and that they're free to stop their involvement at any time;
- an explanation of what will happen and how long it may take;
- an indication of the advantages and disadvantages of participation;
- an assurance of confidentiality and anonymity;
- information about what will be produced at the end;
- information about the funding source;
- the names of the lead researcher and all assistants;
- information about any sponsorship or affiliation connected to the project;
- details of how to claim expenses, if applicable.

There are often set templates that can be used but this isn't always satisfactory because the terminology, format and layout may not be clear for non-specialists. All the information you give out should be brief and expressed in ways that can be easily understood by everyone.

After you've told them what's involved, participants usually sign an 'Informed Consent Form'. They may also have to fill in a debriefing form once the data-gathering phase is over.

---

### brilliant example

Let's assume your research is in medicine and you need to question patients about their treatments. You've gone through the necessary ethical applications and have the committee's approval. But it's still possible for your work to be unethical, even though you don't want or intend it to be. For example, patients are vulnerable and they may feel pressured into taking part but they're afraid to say so because they think they'll get better treatment if they cooperate with you. The research design and consent forms you create must show that you're aware of such possibilities.

---

You must promise all human participants that their identities won't be revealed verbally or in any printed material that comes out of the research. If you think you might

> you must promise all human participants that their identities won't be revealed

want to quote directly from their responses to questions or in focus groups, you must get their permission in writing to do so and reassure them that they'll be quoted anonymously.

### Getting ethical approval

Read the guidance notes from the ethics committee or your department before you start writing your proposal. The format you use for it will depend on your university's preferences. Broadly speaking, you'll need to provide information on:

- the title, purpose and duration of the project, and where it'll take place;
- your methodological approach, and information on how data will be stored securely;
- the way in which you'll recruit volunteers if they're needed, how old they'll be, their gender and any criteria for including or excluding individuals;
- the measures you've taken to cover all ethical dimensions and comply with the appropriate research code of practice in your institution, including confidentiality in reporting results; and
- if appropriate, the name of any funding body.

**brilliant** tip

Don't forget, when you're organising your overall research schedule, to allow time for this process of getting ethical approval. Your supervisor may be able to give you an idea of how long it usually takes. While you're waiting, you can get on with some other aspect of the work, such as a literature review.

## Data protection

The storage and use of personal information is an ethical issue, too. In the UK, the Data Protection Act outlines what is and isn't allowed. If you plan to store information either in paper files or electronically, check your university's web pages for information and guidance. And, even without the pressure of legislation, it's good practice to limit the length of time you'll hold on to data and to tell participants how you'll be storing their data and when you'll delete or destroy it.

# What next?

### Look at websites ...

... for learned societies in your discipline to get the latest information about ethical issues. Apart from helping you to prepare your application for approval, it may be useful if there's an oral exam on your research project and your external examiner wants to explore its ethics in the wider context of the discipline.

### Do some brainstorming ...

... focusing specifically on the ethical dimensions of your research. Write out your title, add major branches for harm, consent and confidentiality, then elaborate on them and any others that occur to you.

### Get to know the ethics guidelines ...

... for research activity in your specialist field. It'll help your personal development and will be part of your professional practice after you graduate.

**brilliant** recap

- Find out the ethical codes and principles which apply in your research area.

- If your work needs to be approved by an ethics committee, prepare your submission with care, spelling out the nature of the work and what you'll expect from participants.

- Obtain consent from and promise confidentiality to everyone involved in your research.

- Follow the rules on data protection.

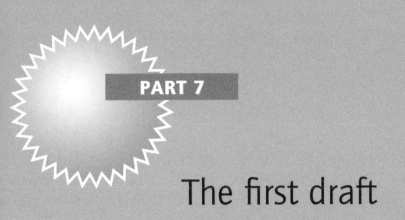

**PART 7**

# The first draft

**CHAPTER 20**

# Structuring your dissertation

Whichever type of writing assignment you've been set, you'll structure it according to a basic format by starting with the general (the introduction), moving on to the specific (the main body) and then moving back again to the general (the conclusion). We're going to look at this structure and examine its elements in more detail.

## The basic format

the standard framework is introduction, main body, conclusion

Let's look first at the standard framework of introduction, main body, conclusion, and suggest how you might organise your writing within it. We'll survey some other academic formats in the next chapter.

### Introduction

This is the first contact your reader makes with you, so you want to create a good impression. It needs to be clear, organised and tell him what to expect in the pages that follow. It gives him an idea of how you handle language and helps him to focus on what you're going to write and the direction in which you'll be taking him. So, in overall terms, it needs to do three things:

1 give a brief general explanation of the topic and its context;

2 outline what you understand it to mean;

3 describe how you're going to approach it.

Part of the third point may be that you warn the reader that you'll be concentrating on certain aspects of the subject rather than giving an exhaustive account of all of it. This may be because it's a complex issue and, if you're having to work to a word limit, you can't do justice to all its aspects. Whatever the reason, it's important to indicate this to the reader/marker so that he understands exactly what to expect and why. You can acknowledge that there are many strands to the topic but explain that you're going to focus on what you consider to be the important ones in the context of the question.

When you've finished writing the assignment, revisit your introduction to make sure it's still an accurate description of what you've actually done. As you write the main body of the text, new ideas often occur and it's easy to get drawn into exploring them. This is fine but you need to alter the introduction to accommodate them.

## brilliant tip

You may have a good idea of what your argument will be but, until you've written the whole text, you can't be absolutely sure of the points you'll make or the balance you achieve between them. For this reason, it might help you to leave the introduction until you've written the main body of your assignment. Once you know what you've said, you'll find it much easier to introduce it. So, if you're struggling with the introduction, consider a different writing sequence: main body, conclusion, introduction.

## Main body

This section consists of all the points you'll be making in your argument and presentation of the materials. Its structure indicates how you're organising the content. As you move from point to point, you may need to generalise, describe, define or give examples as part of your analysis. Try to be as clear and brief as you can, and always keep the reader with you by giving plenty of indications (using signpost words) of any changes of direction, the introduction of new themes or opposing arguments.

As you're writing your first draft, you may find sub-headings useful. They help to keep you focused on exactly where you are in the development of your argument and stop you wandering off the point or getting out of sequence. In most disciplines, they're not acceptable in the final draft which you hand in, but that's not a problem because you can replace them with a topic sentence, which will act as a link with the previous paragraph or an indication of a change of emphasis or direction.

## Conclusion

This summarises everything that's gone before. It ties up any loose ends and reminds the reader of where he's been and what the main conclusions are. Once again, this section can consist of three elements:

1 a reminder of the question and the important features on which you've concentrated;

2 a summary of the specific evidence you've presented to support your views;

3 a statement of your overall viewpoint.

Its function is obviously different from that of the introduction but so is its language. In the introduction, you should try to be clear and avoid jargon or technical words as far as possible. But, since you've probably used technical or more sophisticated terms in the main body as you looked at the subject in more detail, it's appropriate to use that more complex terminology in the conclusion. Don't introduce any new ideas at this stage; your conclusion should be a distillation of the points you've covered in the main body.

Sometimes students rush their conclusion. It might be because there are other things they have to do, or they're fed up with the subject, or they're tired or perhaps just relieved to be near the end of it. Resist this temptation. The conclusion is the thing that creates the final impression in the mind of your reader/marker. Give it your full attention and leave some time after you've written it to look back over it and check that it's correct and has the impact you want.

## brilliant tip

As you're writing, you'll get absorbed in each stage of the argument and its presentation. The points you're making will be very clear to you but when you move to the next point, that takes over and, when you get to the end, you won't have such a clear idea of each step you've taken. So, at the end of each phase of your argument, try jotting down its main ideas and your 'mini-conclusions' about them. If you write them on a separate piece of paper, you'll have a ready-made outline of the main body which will be the perfect plan of your overall conclusion.

## Keep the right balance

It would obviously be absurd to have an introduction which covered the same number of pages as the main body, or a conclusion consisting of three lines. The most substantial (and longest) element of your writing should, of course, be the main body. There are no hard and fast rules about the length of the introduction or conclusion but they should be as short as you can reasonably make them without leaving out essential information. It's all too easy to sweat over the introduction and spend time outlining the context and anticipating points, and then leaving yourself too little time and space to deal with the main body of the

**keep the proportions right**

dissertation itself and the conclusion. Keep the proportions right.

## Word limits

Tutors set word limits not to save them having to mark acres of text but to train you to be precise and concise in your writing. The limit forces you to analyse the topic more carefully to decide what to keep in and what to leave out.

Falling short of the word limit is just as bad as going over it. Some students keep a running total of words they've used and as soon as they reach the minimum required, they stop abruptly. This is not a good approach. It unbalances the overall piece and simply gives the impression that you've run out of ideas. The ending's poor and many points may be left unresolved.

Word count shouldn't really feature when you're writing your first draft. Make it part of the reviewing and editing process. That's when you cut and reshape your writing to make it tighter and clearer.

It's always better to write too much and then have to cut than to write too little and try to pad it out. If your text is seriously past the limit, it might be possible to make an appendix. You could choose some elements to cut, then shorten them and reformat them as bullet points. They're still included in the word count but bullet pointing them makes them shorter. You can then add them to the end as an appendix (or, if there's more than one, several appendices). All it needs is a note in the main body telling the reader that there's further information on a particular point in appendix A (or whichever the relevant appendix is). Before trying this, though, make sure it's acceptable in your department. Check your course handbook or ask a member of staff.

Another way in which you can reduce the count is by thinking about citations. You're expected to include references to publications or experts in your field of study. In law, this could be cases; in the arts and humanities, it could be work by a distinguished academic. But you don't have to quote long pieces of text. Summarise their ideas in your own words (but make sure you acknowledge your source). It's all part of developing the necessary writing skills and techniques.

**brilliant** tip

Most word processors count the words for you. Microsoft Word also has a 'floating' toolbar which shows the total as you write or edit. To access it, go to the Tools menu and choose Tools > Word Count > Show Toolbar. But be careful; looking at it after every few sentences wastes time.

## What next?

### To help you get the right balance ...
... in your writing, look at chapters in textbooks and see how much space they give to introducing the chapter and drawing conclusions.

### Take a piece of your own writing ...
... or a textbook which has sub-headings and practise converting them into topic sentences. Decide which is more effective – the topic sentence or the original sub-heading – and think about why you chose one rather than the other.

### Look at some of your own old ...
... or even recent work and try to identify whether you've included the basic elements and sub-elements of the standard writing format we've identified. Is there a clear division between the introduction, main body and conclusion? What's the balance like between them? Does the introduction cover context, specific focus and statement of intent? Does the conclusion state your

position clearly with the reasons why you've arrived at it? If any of the answers is 'no', work out how you could improve things. It's all part of improving your own writing (and thinking) style.

## brilliant recap

- Understand the basic elements of academic structure – introduction, main body, conclusion – and how they work together.

- Keep the right balance between them.

- Try to be as close to the required word count as possible but leave any necessary cutting until the final draft.

CHAPTER 21

# Structuring
# your report

Reports are supposed to convey information, usually on a clearly defined topic. It's obviously important for you to find and organise that information using sound research techniques and critical thinking, but the way in which you present it can make a significant difference to your assessment. The format you need to use to structure your report may very well be defined by your department or the discipline itself. If that's the case, follow the guidelines closely and group the information in the correct sub-sections.

## Choosing and shaping your content

It can take a long time to gather the material you need for a report – on the internet, in the library, the laboratory or the field – but right from the start, you should have an idea of the style and format you'll be using. You may also need to write up aspects of your findings as you go along, so it's worth fixing a sort of template in your mind. What we'll do here is look at some common formats for scientific project reports, literature surveys and business-style reports.

> right from the start, you should have an idea of the style and format you'll be using

## General skills

As you prepare and present your report, you'll need to call on several skills to cover different phases and activities:

- Description, for reporting your experiments and/or summarising facts.
- Illustration, to organise your findings in diagrams, flow charts, graphs or tables.
- Analysis, to consider your results and maybe to work out descriptive or hypothesis-testing statistics.
- Discussion, to look at all aspects of a position, for and against.
- Solution(s), to explain different possible solutions to problems or issues.
- Evaluation, to help you to decide what's important and why.
- Recommendation, to choose the best solution on the basis of the evidence.
- Conclusion, to say what your research has shown.

## Possible designs

### Literature review

The structure here is simple – title page, abstract, introduction, main body of text, conclusions, references or literature cited. The bulk of the report is contained in the main body which may be sub-divided into sections with sub-headings. They deal with how you chose and analysed your various sources. Be careful how you cite your literature references and present quotes from them. Follow the rules, be consistent and show that you can work within formal academic structures.

### General scientific report

The pattern here is title page, abstract, abbreviations, introduction, materials and methods, results, discussion, acknowledgements, references. It focuses on materials and methods but in some disciplines the order of these components may change. A chemistry report, for example, could consist of title page, abstract, abbreviations, introduction, results, discussion, materials and methods, acknowledgements, references.

## brilliant tip

A scientific report should:

- help the reader to understand and absorb its findings quickly, and cite sources so that he can check them easily if he wants to follow them up;

- give enough detailed information for another competent scientist to repeat the work;

- be objective, balanced and consider all possible interpretations of its results;

- include the appropriate statistical analysis.

### Non-scientific style

Again, this is relatively simple, with title page, introduction, main body of text, and conclusion. There's no focus on materials and methods, but the topic's considered at length in the main body of text. It might be a case study, project or group problem-solving exercise. The SPSER model we described in Chapter 5 might help here – situation, problem, solution, evaluation, (optional) recommendation. You can adapt the headings and sub-headings to fit your particular topic and approach.

### Undergraduate lab reports

These are submitted in earlier parts of courses and probably take the form of a stripped-down and shorter version of the general scientific format, using title page, introduction, materials and methods, discussion/conclusions.

*Business style*

There are some slightly different elements involved here – title page, executive summary, acknowledgements, table of contents, main body of text, bibliography/references, appendices, glossary. The two main differences are that you need to draw conclusions and/or make recommendations in the main body and provide an executive summary. You can also use headings and sub-headings to help the reader to find what she's looking for. The appendices and glossary would help non-specialists to understand the material more easily.

The main aim of this type of report is to provide information that helps decision-making. They're perhaps less formal and the main thing to consider is who you're writing them for.

- A report for a shop-floor manager might be relatively short and informal, and concentrate on production statistics.

- A business plan aimed at an investor or bank manager might again be fairly brief and would focus on financial projections given in charts and tables.

- An academic analysis of a business sector would probably be much longer and more formal, quoting many sources and views.

## brilliant tip

Report writing is an important discipline, with many perhaps surprising benefits. There's the satisfaction of completing a research task successfully and the fact that you've created a record which can be used to repeat or develop your results for future research. But, beyond that, it teaches you the value of organising and presenting your work and thoughts to make them accessible to readers and helps you to develop important professional skills which will make you more employable.

## Typical components

For the sake of simplicity, we've arranged these components in alphabetical order and not in the order they might appear in your report design. The important thing to remember is to check exactly how your department defines them and follow their guidelines to the letter.

follow guidelines to the letter

### Abbreviations

A list of any abbreviations for technical terms used in the text (for example, 'DNA: deoxyribonucleic acid'). It's also customary to include these in the text where you first introduce them, for example 'deoxyribonucleic acid (DNA)'.

### Abstract

A brief summary of the aims of the experiment(s) or observations, the main outcomes and conclusions. This is so that a reader can quickly see and understand your main findings and what you think they mean. It's usually written after you've finished writing the report but it appears at the beginning.

### Acknowledgements

A list of the people who've helped you and whom you would like to thank.

### Appendix (plural appendices)

These can be used for various purposes. They might include tables of information that give detailed breakdowns of some findings and observations and might be consulted by an expert. You can also use them to show such things as a questionnaire template. Basically, appendices are used for data or results that might disrupt the flow of the report or make the results section too long.

*Bibliography/references/literature cited*

This is an alphabetical list of all the sources you've cited in the text. Make sure they follow one of the standard academic formats and that you use it consistently.

*Discussion (or conclusions) – scientific style*

This presents your results and outlines your main conclusions. It could include any or all of the following:

● comments on your methods;

● sources of errors;

● conclusions from a statistical analysis;

● comparison with other findings or the 'ideal' result;

● reflections on what the result means;

● thoughts on how you might improve the experiment;

● recommendations on how you might implement the findings (in a business report);

● an indication of what the next phase might be if you had more time and resources.

You might combine the results and discussions sections to create a more fluid approach to the 'story' of the project, indicating, for example, how one result led to another experiment or approach. Original thinking here could have a significant impact on the marks you get.

*Discussion (or conclusions) – non-scientific style*

This may seem to be a looser construction but it's still important to be thorough, systematic and accurate. You might restate the problem or issue you're dealing with, outline the main solutions or responses to it, and explain why you prefer the one you've chosen, making sure that you support it with appropriate evidence. Sometimes, you may also be asked to make recommendations.

## Executive summary

This takes the place of an abstract in a business report and outlines the key points, usually on a single A4 page. It should start with a brief statement of your aims, followed by a summary of the main findings and/or conclusions, which you might list as bullet points. It ends with a short summary of the main conclusions and/or recommendations. As with an abstract, it's usually written last.

## Experimental

This is a straightforward description of the apparatus and method you've used. It's similar to materials and methods.

## Glossary

Here's where you make a list of terms that might be unfamiliar to the reader and say what they mean.

## Introduction – scientific style

This outlines the background to the project, the aims of its experiments and a brief discussion of the techniques you'll be using. The idea is to let the reader know where she is and help her to understand what you're doing and why you're doing it.

## Introduction – non-scientific style

This sets the study in its context and spells out the specific problem or issue you'll be dealing with. Basically, it's saying what the aims of the report are. You may need to refer to the literature or other resource material you're using.

## Main body of text

As the name suggests, this is where you get to grips with the topic. You spell out your intentions and systematically go through all the relevant solutions or issues which arise, giving a full analysis and supporting it with evidence. You may want to sub-divide it into sections for the sake of clarity. In a scientific literature survey, you might give a chronological account of developments in the field, quoting authors, their ideas and findings.

## Materials and methods

This is a full description of how you set about the various tasks and what you did. Give plenty of detail because it's important that other competent persons should be able to repeat your work.

## Results

Here you describe your experiments and the results you got. Usually these are presented as tables or some form of graphic, but don't use both for the same data – that could be confusing. Highlight any aspects of the data you think are particularly meaningful. By the way, you can organise the data in the way that best suits your argument; you don't have to present it in the same order in which you did the work.

## Table of contents

This is self-explanatory and more likely to be used when the report is quite long. It's effectively an index which lets the reader find the bits which interest him. It may also include a table of diagrams.

## Title page

This should carry the full name(s) of the author(s), the module title, code or course of study, and the date. If it's a business report it may also have the company logo, client details and its classification (for example, 'confidential'). In scientific-style reports, the title is usually descriptive and says what's been done, notes any restrictions, and sometimes describes the main finding. In non-scientific-style reports, it's a brief but comprehensive title that defines the topic.

## brilliant dos and don'ts

### Do

✔ find a model for the type of layout you need. There might be one in your course handbook or you could adapt your own from something you thought was well organised or from the examples we've given.

✔ be aware of your writing style. Reports can be full of details and quite hard to read. Make the reader feel comfortable by using bullet points to break up the text and by keeping your sentences relatively simple and your paragraphs short.

✔ choose the right sort of charts and vary them if you can. Keep all your diagrams and graphs simple and, for all of them, use a title and legend to explain what they're about.

✔ think about what your conclusions may be from an early stage. It may help you to shape how you work and what you look for. But if the evidence starts suggesting it might be wiser to change direction, keep an open mind and don't hesitate to re-examine your choices.

### Don't

✘ include anything that's irrelevant. Your report should be short and to the point. You may have taken ages finding a particular piece of information or analysing something but that's not a reason for keeping it in if it doesn't contribute to your case.

# What next?

**Look again ...**

... at the different types of report we listed earlier and note their similarities and differences. You can compare them with any specific format you've been asked to adopt to check how best to make it work for you.

**If you're writing …**

… a business or scientific report, look at the different types of graph available which might add variety and impact to it. We covered several examples in Chapter 16 but you can find more options in Microsoft Excel's 'Chart Wizard'.

**Remember the importance of …**

… higher-level academic thinking skills. In most forms of report, you'll be assessed on your analysis and evaluation of the material you've collected and how you use it to summarise the topic.

**brilliant** recap

- Before you start, decide which style and format of report you're using – literature review, scientific, non-scientific, lab or business report.

- Use the examples we give to check their component parts and identify the best design for your needs.

- Make your writing easy to read, keep it relevant.

- Form an early idea of your possible conclusions but always be ready to change them.

**CHAPTER 22**

# Academic writing

As we warned in the introduction, the book you're reading is definitely NOT written in an academic style. Its aim is to be more or less conversational, addressing you personally and using contractions (you're, we've, this'll) to create a fairly relaxed reading experience. Academic writing has its own aims and the appropriate conventions to help to achieve them. Success will depend upon you recognising those conventions and learning how to use them. So now we'll attempt to define the basic aspects of academic style and language and suggest what you should and shouldn't do.

## Academic language and conventions

Your present task involves perhaps the most extended piece of academic writing you've ever had to do and so it's even more important that you show you're capable of producing a submission in the appropriate style. There'll be some differences between writing about 'scientific' and 'humanities' subjects but the basics of academic convention are common to both and that's what we'll focus on.

### Academic style

As soon as they hear the words 'academic style' many people immediately assume that it means convoluted sentences, long words and boredom. That may be true of the worst types of academic writing, but it's a false assumption. Basically, academic style aims to use language precisely and objectively to express ideas. It must be grammatically correct, and it's more formal than the styles you find in novels, newspapers, emails, texts and everyday conversation. But it still aims to be clear and simple. Most of all, it avoids illogical or emotionally charged expressions and presents its findings objectively. Its tone is impersonal, its vocabulary succinct and 'correct'.

> academic style aims to use language precisely and objectively to express ideas

### brilliant tip

The academic world thrives on sharing research and learning and there's an old gag that says that the USA and Britain are 'two countries divided by a single language'. Academic writing in the UK is nearly always in British English (BE) but you'll probably read lots of material written in American English (AE). The obvious differences are in spelling – 'colour' (BE) and 'color' (AE) – but there are also differences in vocabulary. In the USA, your 'lecturer' (BE) is your 'professor' (AE) and an author may write 'we have gotten results' (AE) rather than 'we have obtained results' (BE). Some disciplines are trying to standardise their terminology. In chemistry, for example, 'sulphur' (BE) is now spelt 'sulfur' (AE) on both sides of the Atlantic. The differences don't pose a problem but you should be aware of them.

### The need to be objective

However enthusiastic you are about a subject, you mustn't let your personal feelings show through. Apart from anything else, they might cloud your reasoning and create an impression of bias when what you're supposed to be doing is presenting a reasoned, balanced analysis or report. The important thing is the substance of your argument therefore you need to use impersonal language. So don't use personal pronouns, i.e. words such as I, me, you, we, us, and use the passive rather than the active voice. In other words, write about the action, not about who's doing whatever it is.

> you need to use impersonal language

To make this clearer, let's give some examples.

- 'Pressure was applied to the wound to stem the bleeding' is passive.
- 'We applied pressure to the wound to stem the bleeding' is active.
- 'The results were compared with those of the previous experiment' is passive.
- 'I compared the results with those of the previous experiment' is active.

In each case, the second example may seem clearer, more 'natural', but you could also argue that starting with 'we' or 'I' puts the emphasis on who's doing it rather than on the action. By getting rid of 'we' or 'I', the passive construction keeps the emphasis clinical, dispassionate, factual.

You can also achieve that sort of objectivity by changing the verb in the sentence to a noun, so that:

'I **applied** pressure to the wound to stem the bleeding'

becomes:

'The **application** of pressure to the wound stemmed the bleeding'

and

'We **compared** the results with those of the previous experiment' becomes:

> 'A **comparison** was made with the results of the previous experiment.

(In each case, the noun and verb are in bold.)

There are also other ways of maintaining an impersonal style. For general statements, you can use a structure such as 'it is ...', 'there is ...' or 'there are ...' to introduce sentences. But be careful. Look, for instance at this sequence:

> 'Statistics show that survival rates amongst casualties are higher when the preferred treatment is amputation.
>
> It is important for the patient to ...'

The 'it' at the beginning of the new paragraph seems to refer to the word 'amputation', which is very misleading. A new paragraph should introduce a new point. To avoid this, you need to change the sentence round and perhaps begin the new paragraph with 'The important point for the patient is to ...'

The same potential for misunderstanding also occurs when you use 'this is ...' or 'these are ...'; 'that is ...' or 'those are ...'. Words like 'it', 'this', 'these', 'that' or 'those' often refer to words, objects or ideas in preceding sentences. When you use them, make sure there's no ambiguity about their meaning.

### Using the right tense

You should always use the past tense to describe or comment on things that have already happened. In everyday speech we often use the 'wrong' tense, for effect or to add drama or immediacy to a description of something that's happened. Imagine there'd been an incident the previous evening. It would be quite normal to hear someone describing it in this way:

> 'He's standing there and I'm wondering what he's going to do. Then suddenly, he gets in his car and drives off.'

However dramatic the events you may be describing in an academic exercise, you must avoid allowing these habits to creep in. If you were writing a TV documentary, it would be fine for the voice-over to say 'Napoleon orders his troops to advance on Moscow. The severe winter closes in on them and only a few of them manage to survive and return home'. But if it's an academic essay, it must read as 'Napoleon *ordered* his troops to advance on Moscow. The severe winter *closed* in on them and only a few of them *managed* to survive and return home'.

There are times when the present tense obviously is appropriate. When you're describing your results in a report, for example, you'd write 'Figure 5 shows ...' rather than 'Figure 5 showed ...'.

## Using the right words

Good academic writers think carefully about their choice of words. They're looking for precision; they want their meaning to be clear, unambiguous. In colloquial language, we're usually happy to be approximate with our meanings. Take the way we use two-word verbs, for example. What does the verb 'turn down' mean? You can turn down your collar, turn down a side street, turn down the volume, turn down an offer, turn down the radio, turn down the bedcover. And the same applies to almost all such verbs – run over, look up, make up, and so on. They're called phrasal verbs and they have several meanings, some of them surprisingly remote from one another. (You can make up a story and make up someone's face.) It's the sort of looseness that's dangerous in academic writing and you should always try to find a word that leaves no space for misinterpretation.

**brilliant** tip

Quite rightly, there have been questions about how to use gender-specific language. In the past, it was almost always he, him and his.

▶

We said in the introduction how we intended to avoid the problems this causes by using he, she, him, her, his and so on in an arbitrary way. If you don't, and you try to be politically correct all the time, you end up with sentences such as:

> A lecturer must give himself or herself time to prepare his or her lectures so that he or she can be confident that his or her meaning is clear to his or her students.

That's awful. But just as bad is the 'S/he will provide specimens for her/his exam' format. One way round it is to make the sentence plural as in:

> Lecturers must give themselves time to prepare their lectures so that they can be confident that their meaning is clear to their students.

Whichever technique you use, it's important to be aware of the need to remain correct but without creating constructions which are so clumsy that they actually get in the way of meaning.

### From non-academic to academic

Let's see how to change a non-academic text into one that's academically acceptable. At first it reads:

> In this country, we've changed the law so that the King or Queen is less powerful since the Great War. But he or she can still advise, encourage or warn the Prime Minister if they want.

The points that need correcting are as follows:

- 'this country' isn't specific;
- 'we've' is a personal pronoun with a verb that's been contracted;
- 'but' is a connecting word and shouldn't be used to start a sentence, so the grammar's weak;

- the word 'law' is imprecise because it has several meanings;
- 'King or Queen' duplicates nouns;
- 'he or she' and 'they' are pronouns which don't relate properly to one another and are misleading;
- 'can still' is an example of informal style.

If we correct these flaws, we get a much tighter, more focused text:

In the United Kingdom, legislation has been a factor in the decline of the role of the monarchy in the period since the Great War. Nevertheless, the monarchy has survived and, thus, the monarch continues to exercise the right to advise, encourage and warn the Prime Minister.

The changes are:

- 'the United Kingdom' is more specific;
- 'legislation has' is impersonal;
- 'nevertheless' is a powerful signpost word;
- 'legislation' is tighter than 'law';
- 'monarchy' is a singular abstract term;
- 'monarch' replaces the duplication of 'King or Queen';
- 'continues to exercise' illustrates the more formal style.

## The fundamentals of academic writing.

We're going to look at some elements of academic (and non-academic) writing that can cause or maybe help you to overcome difficulties. In a way, they constitute a series of Brilliant dos and don'ts but it might be confusing to mix them together so, instead, we're organising them as an alphabetical list.

### Abbreviations and acronyms

Some abbreviations can be used in academic writing, for example those that express units, such as °C, $m^2$, or km/h, but avoid abbreviations such as e.g., i.e., viz. in formal work. They're fine, however, for note-taking.

Acronyms are a different form of abbreviation. They take the initial letters of an organisation, a procedure or an apparatus and use them as words in their own right. So instead of writing out the World Health Organisation in full every time, you write WHO. The academic convention is that the first time that you use the name of one of these organisations or procedures in your text, you write it in full with the abbreviation in brackets immediately after it. After that, in the same document, it's sufficient to use the abbreviated form. For example: The European Free Trade Association (EFTA) has close links with the European Community (EC). Both EFTA and the EC require new members to have membership of the Council of Europe as a prerequisite for admission to their organisations.

Sometimes, for example in formal reports, as well as using them in this way, you may need to include a list of abbreviations.

### 'Absolute' terms

Be careful when using absolute terms such as always, never, most, all, least and none. You can use them but only when you really are absolutely certain of what you're claiming.

### Clichés

Languages are constantly developing and expressions come and go. Clichés are examples of language which may be useful but which sometimes have become so familiar that they're used without really thinking what they mean. So be aware of when you use them and, where possible, replace them with something less general or less long-winded. For example:

> First and foremost (first); last but not least (finally); at this point in time (now). This procedure is the gold standard of hip replacement methods. (This procedure is the best hip replacement method.)

In that last example, 'gold standard' is an absurd, counter-productive term. It would perhaps be acceptable in a financial context but has no place in a surgical procedure.

## Colloquial language

We've already mentioned this, and we might stress again at this point that the book you're reading is breaking most of the rules we're describing. But, again (See? We began a sentence with 'But'), that's because we're deliberately using a colloquial style. It has no place in an academic paper. Nor has a sentence such as: 'Not to beat about the bush, increasing income tax did the Chancellor no good at the end of the day and he was ditched at the next Cabinet reshuffle'. A far more acceptable version would be: 'Increasing income tax did not help the Chancellor and he was replaced at the next Cabinet reshuffle'. Colloquial language is vibrant, expressive but it has no place in sober academic discourse.

## 'Hedging' language

We keep stressing the need for academic language to be precise. There are times, though, when it's impossible to say definitely that something is or is not the case. That's when you can use verbs that allow you to hedge your bets. In other words, you can state something without subscribing to either side of the argument in question or present several different viewpoints without committing yourself to any particular one of them. That's what we're calling 'hedging' language.

It's very simple; you present the reader with a construction which makes them feel that you're suggesting a hypothetical, or imaginary, case. And you do this by using expressions such as 'it seems that ...', 'it looks as if ...', 'the evidence suggests that ...' and so on. You're not committing yourself, but you're suggesting that something is possible, maybe even probable.

You can actually take it a stage further, too, by using verbs known as modal verbs – can/cannot, could/could not, may/may not, might/might not. If you use them with other verbs they actually increase the sense of uncertainty. For example: 'These results suggest that there has been a decline in herring stocks in the North Sea' can be made even more tentative by saying 'These results could suggest that there has been a decline in herring stocks in the North Sea'.

### Jargon and specialist terms

Jargon can be impenetrable. Some of that used in the commercial world seems fine to begin with but rapidly loses its impact through overuse. In academic disciplines, however, jargon doesn't always have the same pejorative associations. Subjects use language in a way that's exclusive to their particular discipline and students quickly adopt the terminology because it describes objects, systems, ideas and events very precisely. However, it's wise to be aware when you're using terms which might be described as jargon and which might not be understood by non-specialists. In such cases, you should explain the terms. Apart from anything else, it helps you to be sure that you understand them yourself and know how to use them in context.

### Rhetorical questions

As the word 'rhetorical' suggests, these are powerful linguistic weapons when it comes to delivering speeches, They can be useful in academic writing but they should be used with care and not too frequently. If you're in any doubt, don't use them but instead turn them into a statement. For example: 'How do plants survive in dry weather?' becomes 'It is important to understand how plants survive in dry weather'. (And, of course, since it's not a question any more, there's no question mark.)

### Split infinitives

The mission of the Starship Enterprise is 'to boldly go where no no-one has gone before'. That's perhaps the most famous of all split infinitives. The infinitive of any verb is the 'to ...' bit and consists of two words – to eat, to dance, to go – and splitting them means putting another word (usually an adverb) between them. The 'correct' version would be 'to go boldly'. However, although there are still many who deplore such a 'mistake', it's rapidly becoming accepted. Having said that, academic writing tends always towards the 'correct' so it's probably better to avoid splitting the infinitive in your work.

### Value judgements

We've been stressing the need for an objective, impersonal approach. Value judgements express views rather than facts. If you say that 'Louis XIV was a rabid nationalist' without supporting your claim, you're just voicing your opinion. On the other hand, if you say 'Louis XIV was regarded as a rabid nationalist. This is evident in the nature of his foreign policy where he …' you're distancing yourself from the claim and also providing some evidence to support it.

## Punctuation

Good punctuation isn't just something that fussy people worry about. It's a vital aspect of writing, especially in an academic context, and it helps you to communicate exactly what you mean. More and more, though, corporate logos and the slogans that accompany them are designed to attract attention with unconventional print forms that ignore the correct use of capitals, apostrophes, commas and other punctuation marks. Take these variations of a single group of words:

Visitors car park – means nothing; it's just a list of words.

Visitor's car park – is a car park for a single visitor.

Visitors' car park – is a car park for more than one visitor.

Visitor's car, park! – is a strange instruction to a single visitor to park.

Only the middle two versions make sense. The point is that the only way to know what the words mean is to see the punctuation.

Without it, or with bad punctuation, you lose meaning and your reader becomes confused. It may be OK when you're texting friends but not when you're writing a dissertation or report, so it's worth us explaining how to use some punctuation marks that students frequently get wrong.

> with bad punctuation, you lose meaning

*Apostrophes*

Basically, apostrophes do two things.

- They show that something's missing, e.g. **It's** not a good time to sell the house. **It's** been up for sale for ages. **We'll** need to lower the price.
  In that example, three different expressions have been contracted and the apostrophe indicates the missing letters – **It is** ... **It has** ... **We will** ... or **We shall** ... (But remember, never use contractions in academic writing.)

- They indicate ownership, e.g. **Anne's** dress, the **cat's** whiskers, the **government's** proposals.

We need to develop this a little more, though. The examples we've given are for normal, regular words, but there are exceptions.

- As we've seen, for singular nouns, it's easy: you add 's to the end. If they're plural, you just put the apostrophe after the word. 'The **student's** question' means it was asked by one student, 'The **students'** question' means that several students asked it.

- When plurals don't end in s, you need to put **'s** at the end of the word – **men's** habits, **children's** toys, **women's** concerns.

- If more than one person owns something, the second noun takes the apostrophe – Laurel and **Hardy's** comedy is timeless.

- If there are several people who own different things, you need an apostrophe on each one – **Professors'**, **lecturers'** and **students'** priorities are rarely the same.

In all of these examples, if you leave out the apostrophe, it's wrong.

Finally, two examples illustrating a common error.

- How much are the **apple's**? (Never use an apostrophe to create a plural – it should just be **apples**.)
- **It's** time to give the cat **it's** food.
  The second **it's** is wrong. It's stands for it is or it has – as in **It's** (i.e. It has) been broken for a long time but **it's** (it is) OK now. When its is a possessive, there's no apostrophe. **It's** time to give the cat **its** food.

### Capital letters

In English, initial capitals are used to name or introduce the following:

- The first letter of the first word of a sentence.
- Proper nouns for roles, names of people, organisations, rivers, mountains, lochs, lakes and place names, e.g. **T**he **P**rime **M**inister attended the meeting of the **N**orth **A**tlantic **T**reaty **O**rganisation in a hotel overlooking **L**ake **G**eneva.
- Days, months, festivals (but not the seasons).
- Titles of books, plays, films, poems, music, TV programmes.

### Colon

This is used in three main ways:

- to introduce a list, either as part of the sentence or in bullet points like this. (Note, however, that here and in some other instances we've ignored correct academic procedure because we should end each bullet point with a semi-colon – it's part of our deliberately informal style.)

- to explain the previous part of the sentence, e.g. The medic recommended a fitness regime: regular exercise, healthy eating, less alcohol and no smoking.

- to give an example, e.g. The quickest response to a catastrophe often comes from charities: Oxfam, Médecins sans Frontières, Live Aid.

## Comma

This is the most frequently used punctuation point and yet mistakes are still made. Its main functions are:

- To separate things in a list, e.g. The member-states that do not support this view are Britain, France, Germany, Portugal and Greece.

- To separate adjectives describing the same noun, e.g. I want that big, expensive, high-spec computer.

- After connecting or signposting words or expressions, e.g. consequently, as a result, however, thus.

- Before joining words such as 'and', 'but', 'or', e.g. She had researched the topic thoroughly, but her analysis was flawed.

- To give more information about the phrase that went before it, e.g. The leader of the group, Dr Joan Jones, was not available for comment. (This could also be written as: Dr Joan Jones, the leader of the group, was not available for comment.)

- In the final example, see how adding commas actually changes the meaning of the sentence. 'The spectators who were not wearing lifejackets were swept downstream' means that only the spectators without lifejackets were swept away and implies that there were others there who were wearing lifejackets and survived. But 'The spectators, who were wearing lifejackets, were swept downstream' means that all the spectators were wearing lifejackets and they were all swept away.

*Ellipsis*

Ellipsis (...) is used to show that one or more words have been left out of a quotation, e.g. The educational value of streaming pupils ... has yet to be demonstrated. The important thing to note is that you must always use just three dots.

## brilliant dos and don'ts

### Don't

✗ say don't. In fact, don't use any contractions. It's all too easy to slip in the occasional 'it's' or 'it isn't'. They belong to spoken English (and a conversational style such as the one we're using in this book) but there's no place for them in academic written English.

✗ use personal pronouns (I, me, you, us) or similar words such as my, your or our. You may need to change the type of language structures you're using and choose instead the passive voice or impersonal expressions such as 'It is possible that ...'.

## Honing your academic style

If you were desperate for a loan and writing to your bank manager, you wouldn't be all matey or use slang or txt-msging. If you were writing a love letter, you wouldn't use impersonal, formal language and the passive voice. Of course not, because the bank manager and the object of your affections would be expecting a particular sort of vocabulary and tone. Well, academic writing is aimed at a particular type of reader, too, and he'll also have his expectations. So think about your audience. Your readers will probably be marking your work; they'll want to see knowledge, content and they'll be looking for evidence of critical thinking and the correct use of specialist terms and structures.

## What next?

### It's very important for your English ...

... to be grammatically correct. If you're not sure whether yours is good, get a grammar book or type 'English grammar' into a search engine and choose a page which presents material in the form you need it.

### Work with a friend ...

... on improving your writing styles. Swap examples of your writing, read hers and get her to read yours critically, then discuss your findings. Talking about them will force you to identify exactly what's right and what's wrong. Feedback's a crucial part of learning and you should get it wherever you can.

### As you read books and articles ...

... notice how the authors use the techniques we've been describing. Look for examples of 'hedging' language and see if there are other ways in which authors manage to avoid making absolute judgements. The more you become aware of these stylistic features, the more naturally they'll come to you in your own work.

**brilliant** recap

- Remember that objectivity, good grammar, the right words, the right style and correct use of punctuation are central to academic writing conventions.

- Understand and learn to handle the potentially problematic elements of academic writing, from abbreviations to value judgements.

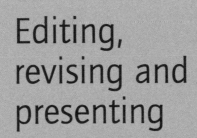

**PART 8**

Editing,
revising and
presenting

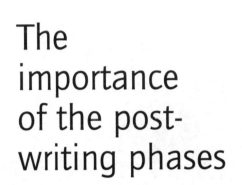

**CHAPTER 23**

# The importance of the post-writing phases

f you want your work to be of the highest quality you can manage (which most people obviously do), you must not only take great care while you're writing it, you must also look at it critically and objectively to pick up and correct any flaws which have crept in. Even with the most meticulous professional writers, grammatical slips, misspellings and typographical errors often go unnoticed. You want to be proud of this piece of work, so be careful with every aspect and phase of its production.

> grammatical slips, misspellings and typographical errors often go unnoticed

## Make your writing make sense

When you've put the final full stop to your first draft, you'll feel a huge sense of relief and just want to hand it in and relax. But the writing of the text is only a part of the overall creative process. The next phase, which consists of reviewing, editing, proofreading and preparing your dissertation or report for final submission, is just as critical and can make a real difference to the finished piece of work. When you draw up your time management schedule at the beginning, try to organise it so that you leave a gap between finishing the writing and starting the editing. That will let you get some distance between you and the work and you'll be able to read it with fresh eyes when you get back to it.

When you do, you'll be looking for lots of things, such as flaws in layout, grammar, punctuation and spelling. You'll be checking to see that it's consistent in its use of terminology and in presentational features such as font and point size, layout of paragraphs, and labelling of tables and diagrams. But you'll also be looking critically at its content to make sure it's relevant and that it makes sense.

It can be a complex process but if you don't do it thoroughly there's little doubt that you'll get fewer marks than you would have if you'd taken some time to make sure you'd got things right. Style, content, structure and presentation all contribute to the clarity and impact of what you're handing in. On top of that, the very act of learning how to edit your work properly will sharpen your powers of critical analysis.

### brilliant definition

**Reviewing** – examining a task or project to make sure it meets the set requirements and objectives and makes overall sense.

**Editing** – revising and correcting a piece of work to arrive at a final version. Usually, this involves focusing on smaller details of punctuation, spelling, grammar and layout.

**Proofreading** – checking a printed copy for errors of any sort.

## Choosing a strategy

How you approach this will depend on your preferences. Some people prefer to go through their text just once, trying to pick up every flaw in all the different areas; others make several passes, looking each time at a different aspect – grammar, spelling, style, and so on. It's up to you to decide what works best for you. At the outset, it might help if you try focusing on each of these three broad aspects in separate sweeps through the text.

*Content, relevance, clarity and coherence*

● Remember, it helps if you read your work aloud.

● Check the title and confirm that you've covered the areas it said you would.

● Check what aims you set out in your introduction and make sure they've been met in your treatment of the subject.

● Be objective as you read, checking that your argument makes sense, your facts are correct and there aren't any inconsistencies.

● Cutting a text by 10–25 per cent can significantly improve its quality, so get rid of anything that's not relevant, any informal language or expressions and any gendered or discriminatory language.

● Double-check that you've acknowledged all your sources. Don't risk plagiarism.

**brilliant** tip

You may be surprised to hear that errors and typos which are missed on the computer screen are often obvious when they're printed out. Always use a printout for your final check. If you still find errors, it's easy enough just to reprint individual pages.

*Grammar, spelling and punctuation*

● Think about how well the text flows and check that the different parts link together. If they don't, add some signpost words to guide the reader along.

● Check the length of your sentences and try to get a balance by mixing long and short.

● Check your spelling with both a spell-checker and, if you're unsure about something, in a standard dictionary.

- If, as you read, you feel that something's clumsy, try rewriting it in different ways, moving the parts of the sentences around, changing active to passive or vice versa or finding synonyms.

- Get rid of any 'absolute' terms which might introduce a note of subjectivity.

**brilliant tip**

Word processors have made reviewing and editing much easier. To make sure you get the most out of them:

- Use the word-count facility.

- Check page breaks and the general layout with the 'View' facility before you print it out.

- Don't rely entirely on the spelling and grammar checker.

- If staff add comments using 'Tools > Track Changes' in Microsoft Word, you can accept or reject them by right-clicking on whatever has been marked for alteration.

*Presentation*

- If you've used titles and subtitles, make them stand out by using either bold or underlining (but not both).

- Make sure you haven't crammed the text into too tight a space, and that it's neat and legible.

- Check that your reference list is complete, consistent with whatever style you've chosen or been told to use, and that all citations are matched by an entry in it and vice versa.

- Make sure you've included your name, matriculation number and course number.

- Number and clip or staple the pages together, with a cover page if needed.

- Go through all diagrams, charts and other visual materials to check that they're in sequence and labelled consistently.

- If there's any supporting material in the form of footnotes, endnotes, appendices or a glossary, make sure they too follow the right sequence.

## brilliant tip

There are universally recognised symbols that are used in proof correcting. They're a sort of shorthand to indicate omissions, misspellings, grammatical mistakes and many other aspects of the text which need attention. Your tutors may use them on your essays and it's useful if you familiarise yourself with them so that you can use them yourself. We've listed the most common ones in Table 23.1 and given examples of how they're used. You can easily find a list of the most common ones and their meanings by simply typing 'proofreading symbols' into a search engine.

## A checklist

It may help you to break the editing down into five main areas that need attention. You can then use them as a checklist and work through them systematically.

### Content and relevance

- Have you said what you meant to say and does it match the title?

- Is the structure you've used right for the task?

- Have you dealt with the topic objectively, using relevant examples?

- Are your facts accurate and have you cited all your sources correctly?

| Correction mark | Meaning | Example |
|---|---|---|
| ⌐ (np) | (new) paragraph | *Text*                                    *margin* |
| ≠ | change CAPITALS to small letters (lower case) | The correction marks that tutors |
| ∼∼∼ | change into **bold** type | use in students' texts are generally    Y |
| ≡ | change into CAPITALS | made to help identify where there |
| ◯ | close up (delete space) | have been errors of spllinor        ʎe ʎg |
| / or ⌐ or ⊢ | delete | punctuation. They can often      (STET) |
| ʎ | insert a word or letter | indicate where there is lack of |
| Y | insert space | paragraphing or grammatical |
| .... or (STET) | leave unchanged | accuracy. If you find that work is    (np) |
| Insert punctuation symbol in a circle (P) | punctuation | returned to you with such marks correction, then it is            ⌐⌐ |
| **plag.** | plagiarism | worthwhile spending some time analysing the common errors as     ⌐ |
| ⟶ | run on (no new paragraph) | well as the comments, because this will help you to improve the |
| **Sp.** | spelling | quality of presentation and content |
| ⌐⌐ | transpose text | of your work this reviewing can    ⊙/≡ have a positive effect on your |
| ? | what do you mean? | assessed mark. |
| ?? | text does not seem to make sense | |
| ✓ | good point/correct | *In the margin, the error symbols are separated by a slash (/).* |
| ✗ | error | |

**Table 23.1 Common proofreading symbols**. University lecturers and tutors use a variety of symbols on students' work to indicate errors, corrections or suggestions. These can apply to punctuation, spelling, presentation or grammar. The symbols provide a kind of 'shorthand' that acts as a code to help you see how you might be able to amend your text so that it reads correctly and fluently. In this table some of the more commonly used correction marks are shown alongside their meanings. The sample text shows how these symbols may be used either in the text or the margin to indicate where a change is recommended.

*Source*: Adapted from Table 1 'Marks for copy preparation and proof correction' BS 5261-2:2005, British Standards Institution.

*Clarity, style and coherence*

- Are the aims and objectives clear?
- Does the text flow, using the right signpost words?
- Have you removed any informal language?
- Is the style academic and right for the task?
- Are content and style consistent throughout?
- Have you used the right tenses and are they consistent?
- Have you achieved the right balance between sections?

*Grammatical correctness*

- Are all sentences complete and do they make sense?
- Have you checked for any grammatical errors which you keep on making?
- Have you been consistent is using British or American English?

*Spelling and punctuation*

- Have you corrected all 'typos'?
- Have you checked the spelling, especially of words that you often misspell?
- Have you also checked the spelling of subject-specific words and foreign words?
- Have you checked punctuation and tried reading aloud?
- Are all proper names capitalised?
- Are any of the sentences too long? If so, try splitting them into smaller ones.

*Presentation*

- Is it close enough to the word-count target?
- Does the work look neat?
- Are the cover-sheet details correct?

- Does your presentation follow departmental requirements?
- Is the bibliography/reference list formatted correctly?
- Have you numbered the pages?
- Are figures and tables in the right format?

## Reminders of the basics

When you're planning a writing assignment, make sure you factor in plenty of time for reviewing and proofreading. You've worked hard on gathering the material and structuring it, so don't spoil it by skimping on this important final stage.

> factor in plenty of time for reviewing and proofreading

Review and edit on paper. That's the way your marker will probably see it and it's the best way to spot errors and inconsistencies. It's also easier to make notes on it and it lets you see the whole work rather than just a screen-sized segment. You can even spread it out on your desk and get an overview of the whole flow of your argument.

Read it aloud. It's a technique used by professionals and it picks up inconsistencies, repetitions, faulty punctuation and lapses in logic in a way that a silent reading doesn't.

Trying mapping your work. By that, we mean take the topic headings from your paragraphs and jot them down in sequence on a separate piece of paper. It'll give you a snapshot of your text and let you check the order, see whether it flows and whether it's sticking to your original plan. And it makes it easier to move parts of your work around if you feel it's necessary.

Compare your introduction and conclusion to make sure they complement rather than contradict one another and follow the thread of your argument to see whether it strays off the point anywhere.

Too many words can be just as bad as too few. The main point is that the writing must be clear to your reader. If that means taking longer to explain something, do it. If it means cutting something you've written, cut it, no matter how wonderful you think the sentences you're discarding are. Remember that cutting almost invariably improves a piece of writing.

Create 'white space'. It makes your work look more 'reader-friendly'. You can do this by leaving space between paragraphs and around diagrams, tables and other visual material and also between headings, sub-headings and text. And if you only justify on the left side of the page, there's more space on the right.

Neat presentation, punctuation and spelling all help your reader to access the information, ideas and argument of your writing. It may not earn you marks but it certainly won't lose you any, whereas a messy presentation may make your text – and therefore your argument – harder to decipher.

## What next?

### Look at a past assignment ...
... and go through it using the checklist. Focus on just a couple of pages and highlight all flaws, inconsistencies or errors and think about how much these may have cost you in terms of marks. This might help convince you that time spent reviewing and editing is time well spent.

### On the same piece of text ...
... practise using the standard proofreading symbols. It'll speed up your proofreading on your next assignment.

### Practise condensing ...
... a segment of the text. Look for irrelevant points, wordy phrases, repetitions and over-long sentences. Try to reduce it by 10–25 per cent and, when you read it, you'll probably see

that you've created a much tighter, easier-to-read, better piece
of writing.

### brilliant recap

- It's important to review, edit and proofread your final draft.
- Choose a strategy which suits you for checking your work.
- Use the checklist broken down into five main areas to help
  you: content and relevance; clarity, style and coherence;
  grammatical correctness; spelling and punctuation;
  presentation.
- Remember the basics of preparing, presenting and submitting
  your work.

**CHAPTER 24**

# Making the most of feedback

Feedback can come in different forms and may vary from one discipline to another. The process of writing a dissertation or a report stretches over a longish period and you'll probably get many comments and suggestions, written and oral, from your supervisor. She may want to look at one or more drafts of your work or sections of it. Whatever type of feedback you get, it's important to learn from it and incorporate those lessons into your approach. In this chapter we'll try to expand and interpret the type of notes that may be written on the drafts you submit.

> whatever type of feedback you get, it's important to learn from it

## Learning from feedback

With essays and other such exercises, you knew how you were doing by the mark or grade they earned, but that doesn't happen with dissertations or project reports. So it's your supervisor's comments which tell you how you're getting on and what remedial action, if any, you need to take.

**brilliant tip**

You can get a less formal and obviously less expert opinion of your work from fellow students or members of your family. They may not know much (or anything) about the subject, but they'll be able to say how clear your writing is or whether your argument is logical or has gaps.

## Types of feedback

We can't really say much here about informal, verbal feedback such as comments made as you work in the lab, or observations on your contribution in a seminar, but they're important so, if you're not sure what they mean, ask about them. Depending on your department's policies, you may be able to arrange a meeting with your supervisor to discuss them.

When you get back drafts you've handed in, they'll probably have handwritten comments on them with maybe an overall summary with suggestions about things you might need to change. There's also the facility in Microsoft Word that you'll find under Tools > Track changes. Your tutor may use this to suggest rewordings or other amendments. Word's comments facility also allows her to add explanations or ideas. If you're not familiar with how this works, check the Help menu.

### brilliant tip

Always read your feedback. It's there to point out specific aspects of your work which are being commended or aren't being handled as effectively as they could be. You should use it to make later submissions better, help to develop your structure and style, and deepen your understanding of the topic. If you ignore points that are made, especially those concerned with presentation or structure, you'll keep on repeating the mistakes and find yourself penalised for them over and over again.

## Some comments and what they mean

Although, as we pointed out in the previous chapter, there's a set of signs which are used when proofreading to indicate various textual problems which need correcting, there isn't an equivalent terminology shared by lecturers and tutors everywhere. If there were, it would imply that both writing and marking are automatic processes with 'right' and 'wrong' answers. Supervisors may use the proofreading symbols as a sort of shorthand but their comments will be personal. So you'll need to get used to interpreting the particular ways they express their opinions. Also, if their habit is to scribble notes as they read, their handwriting may be difficult to decipher. Don't hesitate to ask if you can't understand what's being said.

> don't hesitate to ask if you can't understand what's being said

Usually, comments are written in the right-hand margin or between the relevant lines. The words, phrases, sentences or paragraphs to which they refer are underlined, circled or indicated in some other way. All we can do here is give a few examples of commonly used feedback comments and suggest what they mean and how you should react to them to improve your writing.

*Comments on content*

- **Relevance? Importance? Value of example? So?**
  These suggest that you may have used a quotation that's not right for the context or you maybe haven't explained its relevance. Read your words carefully to test how logical they are and whether the irrelevance is obvious to you. Do you need to explain it further or more clearly? Should perhaps you choose a more appropriate example or quote?

- **Detail. Give more information. Example? Too much detail/waffle/padding**
  You've either not provided enough detail to make your point or there's too much and your point's getting lost. You may also have realised that your argument's a bit thin so you've tried to make it seem better by putting in lots of description rather than analysis.

- **You could have included ... What about ...? Why didn't you ...?**

These obviously indicate that something's missing. You should, by reading through it, see where the gap is and what's needed to fill it.

- **Good! Excellent! ✓(which may recur throughout the work)**
  These are the remarks you want – expressions of approval, confirmation that you're on the right track.

- **Poor. Weak. No! ✗(which may recur throughout the work)**
  And this is what you don't want to see – expressions of disapproval, indications that there's something wrong with your examples, your quotations, your interpretation of them, etc.

*Comments on structure*

- **Logic?** *Non sequitur* **(which means this doesn't naturally follow what preceded it)**
  Your logic or argument is faulty. It may call for you to make quite radical changes to your approach to and analysis of the topic.

- **Where are you going with this? Unclear**
  This suggests that you've failed to introduce the topic clearly or that it's gone off course. Check that you do understand the task properly and know what restrictions there are on your response. Then decide how to tackle the subject.

- **Unbalanced discussion. Weak on pros and cons**
  Once again, it suggests a failure in your logic. When you're comparing and/or contrasting in any way, you must give more or less equal coverage to the pros and cons of the argument.

- **So what? Conclusion?**
  You've failed to conclude clearly. You have to sum up the central features of your writing and shouldn't add any new

material at this point. When you do that properly, it shows that you can think critically and define and highlight the main thread of your argument.

- **Watch out for over-quotation. Too many quotations**
  This means exactly what it says. If you include too many direct quotations from your sources, there's a real danger of plagiarism. You need to synthesise the information and reproduce the ideas in your own words to show that you've understood and absorbed it.

- **Move text (alternatively, loops and arrows may indicate the required changes)**
  Suggestions such as this are usually intended to improve the flow or the logic.

*Comments on presentation*

- **sp. (spelling), (insert material here), (break paragraph here), (delete this material), P (punctuation error)**
  These are indications of minor proofing errors and this is where the proofreading symbols may be used.

- **Citations. Reference (required). Ref? Reference list omitted**
  You've missed out a reference to the original source of an idea, argument or quotation. It's a fault you must correct, otherwise you're once again risking plagiarism. If you provide no reference list, it suggests that there's no solid basis for your work and that you've done no specialist reading.

- **Illegible! Untidy. Can't read**
  Again, this is self-evident. (It can also be ironic in that sometimes the marker's own handwriting is very untidy). You can avoid it by using a word processor.

- **Please follow departmental template for reports. Order!**

If the department or school provides a template for writing reports, you must use it. If you don't, you may lose marks.

**brilliant tip**

Supervisors are busy people and may have several other students. There may also be departmental rules about how many drafts of your work they're allowed to read. On the other hand, they may be willing to look at several drafts as your work progresses. Find out what policy applies in your department and, if you can only submit one draft for checking, make sure it's nearly complete. But whether you can only submit one or several, make sure you get the most out of the reactions and comments you get.

## What next?

### Look up and understand ...

... your department or faculty's assessment criteria. They'll help you interpret feedback and understand how to reach the standard you want to achieve.

### If your feedback comments ...

... are frequently about the same sort of error, concentrate on eliminating it. It may be spelling or grammar or they may suggest you need more examples. Whatever the problem, spend time identifying its exact nature and try to overcome it.

### Give yourself feedback ...

... by reading your work as objectively as possible, sensing where the weaknesses are and tackling them. It's the sort of process that should be happening as you review and edit your work and it's an essential academic skill.

### Learn from the views ...

... of your supervisor. It's often natural to feel that some feedback's unfair, harsh or has misunderstood your approach. But the fact is that supervisors usually have a deeper understanding of the topic than you do and, anyway, the harsh reality is that, if you want to do well in a subject, you'd better find out what constitutes 'good' work and learn how to produce it.

## brilliant recap

- There are various forms of feedback. It's important to take note of them.

- Know how to respond to the different written comments on content, structure and presentation.

**CHAPTER 25**

# The importance of presentation

You're nearly there. You've spent lots of time and effort on collecting and organising material and structuring it to make your argument clear and your conclusions strong and well-supported. You've checked, read and corrected the final draft. After all that, it's worth making sure you present the material in the best possible way to create the right impression on the reader. It's not rocket science to realise that a dog-eared, dirty, coffee-stained bundle of paper won't be viewed in quite the same way as a clean, tidy, professionally prepared document. So it's time for the final pre-submission survey.

## Academic conventions of presentation

The major part of the assessment of your work will focus on two things:

- The things you do *before* you write – researching sources, conducting experiments, analysing the literature.
- How you express your ideas in writing.

But there'll always be some marks awarded for presentation, and how something looks can have a sub-liminal influence on how we judge its quality. The way in which you package and deliver your work reveals the degree of respect for and pride in what you've written and if you seem to care little

> there'll always be some marks awarded for presentation

for it, it doesn't encourage the reader to anticipate anything very special.

We're not just talking about layout and the use of visual elements; we also mean accuracy, consistency and attention to detail. It's part of the proofreading phase, so allow time for it.

## brilliant tip

This really is worth the time you spend on it because:

- It may be part of your assessment.
- It helps the reader to understand what you've written.
- It shows you've taken your work seriously and have a professional approach.
- It demonstrates skills that'll transfer to other subjects and, later, to the job you do.

## Layout

This will depend on the type of academic writing you're producing. Just like an essay, a dissertation could have a relatively simple structure: a cover page, the main essay text and a list of references. A lab report might have title page, abstract, introduction, sections on materials and methods, results, discussion/conclusion and references. There'll be variations, too, according to your academic discipline and maybe even your department. You'll have to find out what's expected of you before you get started on your first assignment. Check your course book or ask your supervisor.

## Cover page

This is the first thing your reader will see, so get it right. If your department has a preferred cover-page design, follow it exactly. It may have been organised that way for a specific administrative purpose, such as making sure that work's marked anonymously or giving markers a standard format for feedback, so stick to the rules.

If there aren't any such rules, put the title in the middle of the page and, in the top right-hand corner or below the title (depending on your department's preferred format), write your name and/or matriculation number. It's also useful for you to add the name of the tutor. The aim is clarity. Don't be tempted to indulge in fancy fonts or graphics; it won't earn you any extra marks.

## Main text

Dissertations and project reports are usually word-processed documents. That gives them a professional look as well as making it easier for you to draft and edit them. Print on just one side of the paper – it makes it easier to read.

### *Font*

There are two main choices: serif types have extra little strokes at the end of each letter; sans serif types don't. It'll probably be up to you to choose your preferred font but serif types with a font size of 11 or 12 are the easiest to read for most people.

Elaborate font types may look attractive or exciting but they can be distracting and actually get in the way of absorbing the content. The same remark applies to using too many forms of emphasis. Choose *italics* or **bold** and stick with the one you've chosen throughout. If you need to add symbols, use Microsoft Word's 'Insert > Symbol' command.

elaborate font types can be distracting

### *Margins*

A useful convention is for left-hand margins to be 4 cm and the right-hand margins 2.5 cm. This leaves space for handwritten comments and makes sure that the text can be read if you use a left-hand binding.

## Line spacing

It's easier to read text spaced at least at 1.5–2 lines apart. Some markers like to add comments as they read the text and this leaves them space to do so. If you're inserting long quotations, though, you should indent them and make them single-line spaced.

## Paragraphs

We've already noted the value of 'white space'. Lay out your paragraphs clearly and consistently. Depending on your department's preferences, you can indent them, which means the first line starts four spaces in from the left-hand margin, or block them, which is when they all begin on the left-hand margin but you separate them by a double-line space. If you choose the indent method, the convention is that the first paragraph is *not* indented. In Microsoft Word you can control your paragraph style using the 'Format > Paragraph' command.

## brilliant tip

If you're not used to using computers for writing, note that you don't have to hit 'return' at the end of each line. When you get to the end of a line, the program automatically 'wraps' your writing onto the next line for you.

## Sub-headings

Sub-headings are useful structural guides for you and your reader. Whether you can use them or not will depend partly on your discipline and your department's policy. In some subjects they're acceptable, even encouraged, but in others they're discouraged. If you're not sure about this, check with your supervisor or look in your course handbook.

*Word count*

Take the word count seriously. Writing too much is as bad as writing too little. If you go way over the limit, the likelihood is that you'll swamp the reader with information and your points may get lost amongst all the words. Almost all writing benefits from being cut.

## Citations and references

It must be clear by now that you must cite authors and sources when you're discussing other people's ideas or quoting from their work. That's why you have to provide a reference list.

A citation is when you mention a source in the main body of your text. You usually note the surname of the author, date of publication and, in some styles, the relevant page(s). You'll give more details about it in the reference, details which, for example, the reader would need if she wanted to find it in a library.

---

### brilliant example

A citation using the Harvard method would read like this:

> According to Smith (2005), there are three reasons why aardvark tongues are long.

And, again using Harvard, the reference would be:

> Smith, J. V., 2005. Investigation of snout and tongue length in the African aardvark (*Orycteropus afer*). *Journal of Mammalian Research*, 34; 101–32.

---

## Quoting numbers in text

The accepted conventions for including numbers in your writing are as follows:

- In general writing, spell out numbers from one to ten but use figures for 11 and above; in formal writing, spell them out from one to a hundred and use figures above that.

- Spell out high numbers that can be written in two words, such as 'six hundred' and when you get into the millions, you can combine figures and spelling. For example: 4,200,000 can also be written as 4.2 million.

- Always use figures for dates, times, currency or to give technical details ('5-amp fuse').

- Always spell out numbers that begin sentences, indefinite numbers ('hundreds of soldiers') or fractions ('seven-eighths').

- Numbers and fractions should be hyphenated, as in 'forty-three' or 'two-thirds'.

## Figures and tables

If you need to use visual material or data to support your arguments, it's important that you do so in a way that best helps the reader to assimilate the information. Once again, there may be rules of presentation that are specific to your subject or department.

### Figures

The term figures ('Fig.' for short) includes graphs, diagrams, charts, sketches, pictures and photographs (although sometimes photographs may be labelled as 'plates'). The guidelines for using them are pretty strict, so it pays to know them.

- You must refer in the text to every figure you use. There are 'standard' wordings for this, such as 'Fig. 4 shows that ...'; or ' ... results for one treatment were higher than for the other (see Fig. 2)'. Find out what system applies in your subject.

- Number the figures in the order in which you refer to them in the text. If you're including the figures themselves within the main body of text (which usually makes things easier for the reader), put them at the next suitable position in the text after the first time you mention them.

- Try to print them at the top or bottom of a page, rather than between blocks of text. It looks neater and makes the text easier to read.
- Each figure should be labelled (the label is called the 'legend'). This'll include the number, a title and some text. The convention is for legends to appear below each figure.

When we were talking about constructing your written arguments, we kept stressing the need for clarity; the same obviously applies here. Make sure, for example, that the different slices of a pie chart or the lines and symbols in a graph are clearly distinguishable from one another. Be consistent by using the same line or shading for the same entity in all your figures. Colour printers are obviously an advantage here but some departments may still insist on black and white images. If you are using colour, keep it 'tasteful' and remember that certain combinations are difficult for some readers to differentiate.

There are technical reasons why some forms of data should be presented in particular ways (for example, proportional data is easier to read in a pie chart than in a line chart), but your main focus should always be on selecting a type of figure that will make it easier for the reader to absorb the information you are giving.

## brilliant tip

If you use integrated suites of office-type software, you can create graphs with the spreadsheet program and insert them directly into your word-processed text. You can even link the two so that, if you

▶

change the spreadsheet data, the change automatically appears in the graph in the text. To find out how this works, consult the manual or 'Help' facility in MS Word. Digital photographs can also be inserted using the 'Insert > Picture > From File' command.

## *Tables*

Tables can summarise large amounts of detailed information, both descriptive and numerical. They generally include a number of columns and rows. Just as with graphs and charts, the convention is to put the categories on the vertical axis (in other words, down the page in the left-hand column), and the variables which are being measured on the horizontal axis (i.e. across the page at the top of the columns). So if we were presenting the data resulting from a survey of attitudes to university teaching, we might have rows for the opinions of students, lecturers, educational experts and the general public, and the columns across the page might be headed 'Positive aspects', 'Negative aspects', 'Value to society', 'Relevance to society'.

### brilliant tip

If you have some data which could be presented as either a figure or a table, which should you choose? Well first of all, never do both. The guiding principle should be to select whichever will be more likely to help the reader assimilate the information. If the message depends on visual impact, a figure might be best; but if details and numerical accuracy are important, a table might be more suitable.

## ⊗ brilliant dos and don'ts

### Do

✔ insert a space after full stops, commas, colons, semi-colons, closing inverted commas (double and single), question marks and exclamation marks.

✔ create one standard line space between paragraphs.

✔ italicise letters for foreign words and titles of books, journals and papers.

✔ format headings in the same font size as the text, but in bold.

✔ use the same figure and table styles that you find in your subject literature.

✔ check your course handbook for specific presentational requirements.

### Don't

✘ choose flamboyance or ostentation. Go for the safe, standard word-processing layout conventions.

✘ justify the text on both sides. Left-justified text creates more 'white space'.

✘ insert a space after apostrophes 'inside' words, e.g. it's, men's, monkey's.

✘ automatically accept the graphical output from spreadsheets and other programs. They may not be in the approved style.

# What next?

## Look at work you've done ...

... in the past to work out the type of presentation that's expected. Ask a student who's done the same sort of work before whether you can look at their submission, or ask your supervisor to show you an example of work that was rated highly. Look for the presentational features we've discussed and think about what you need to do to achieve the same or higher standards.

## Make sure your printed output ...

... is of the highest possible quality. Choose really good quality paper and set the printer to produce its best output. If your own printer isn't good enough, ask to use a friend's or check out the possibilities of using a professional printing service.

## Plan ahead ...

... for everything connected with binding and other aspects of the final presentation. Find out early on whether your department wants dissertations and reports to be bound, and, if so, set time aside for it. Check out local binding services and ask how long the job will take. If binding isn't necessary, buy a high-quality folder.

### brilliant recap

- Follow the prescribed academic conventions of presentation.

- Note the different types of layout for different subjects.

- The main elements of the layout are cover page, main text, font, margins, line spacing, paragraphs, sub-headings, word count, citations and references.

- Quote numbers in texts and use visual elements such as figures and tables.

# Conclusion: Take the advice but be yourself

We've covered a lot of ground and sometimes we've made the same points again and again: the need to avoid plagiarism and the associated importance of identifying and citing all your sources; the need to keep your academic style impersonal; the importance of making objective statements which you can support rather than offering value judgements; and many others. Our intention throughout has been to define the structures you need to work within and help you to know why you're doing things in a particular way.

When you begin to work on your dissertation or report, it can seem daunting, but there's great satisfaction in following an idea and constructing a coherent, well-supported argument to communicate it. Having to work within the apparent constraints of academic conventions may at first seem restrictive but, once you're comfortable with the different requirements, you'll see them as liberating. They'll help you to think more clearly, organise your material, and produce a professional piece of writing that's unique to you and an expression of your own personality.

There's one theme which it's worth singling out for special reference – the need for you to exercise your critical thinking. That's the skill that will be most useful to you in everything you do. Life is far more than surfaces; if that's all you see and understand, you're missing subtleties, complexities, meanings that can change your appreciation of people, society, art, music, literature, commerce, politics, even nature itself. So get inside your studies and let them get inside you, look more deeply into the materials you encounter, be intellectually curious. Don't accept all the information you're bombarded with at its face value: unwrap it, question it, challenge it. Don't be content just to know things; understand them.

# Index